Under the Trade Wind Sky

Under the Trade Wind Sky
Caribbean Adventures and Other Tales of the Sea
Copyright ©2023 by Captain Lou Boudreau

Published in the USA by:
Seaworthy Publications, Inc.
6300 N Wickham Rd.
#130-416
Melbourne, FL 32940
Phone 321-610-3634
email orders@seaworthy.com
www.seaworthy.com
Your Bahamas and Caribbean Cruising Advisory

All rights reserved. No part of this book may be reproduced, stored in a retrieval system, or transmitted in any form, or by any means, electronic, mechanical, photocopying, recording, or by any storage and retrieval system, without permission in writing from the publisher.

Library of Congress Cataloging-in-Publication Data

Names: Boudreau, R. L. (Robert Louis) author.
Title: Under the trade wind sky : Caribbean adventures and other tales of the sea / Captain Lou Boudreau.
Description: Melbourne, FL : Seaworthy Publications, Inc., [2022] | Summary: "Under the Trade Wind Sky is a compilation of tales about growing up and coming of age in one of the most unique ways imaginable, as a sailor on some of the most celebrated sailing yachts of all time. Robert Louis (Lou) Boudreau first went to sea when he was six months old aboard the famous 98-foot schooner Yankee. His father owned and sailed the schooner in the beautiful Bras D'Or Lakes of Cape Breton, Nova Scotia, Canada. When Lou was a year old the Boudreau's left Canada and voyaged south to warmer climes. Sailing out of Miami, Florida, they eventually ran their charter cruises in the West Indies. Lou spent his early childhood on the island of St. Lucia, sailing the Caribbean aboard such vessels as the 100 ft. schooner Doubloon and the 98 ft. Howard Chappelle designed Baltimore clipper Caribee, both owned by his father. In fact, in November of 2022, Lou's father, Capt. Walter Boudreau, was inducted posthumously into the Charter Yacht Brokers Association Hall of Fame for his lifetime achievements in the charter industry. The adventures under sail made a deep and lasting impression on young Lou. In 1968, at age 16, Lou joined the crew of the 135-foot Herreshoff schooner, Ramona, on a voyage to Nova Scotia, and following this, left school to follow the sea permanently. The young seafarer's apprenticeship saw him on some well-known sailing vessels including the 143 ft. schooner Bluenose II and the 137 ft. Herreshoff schooner Le Voyageur. The stories contained herein are a treasure trove of tales about what it was like to sail those famous schooners, priceless childhood stories about growing up in the West Indies, as well as several historical tales of seamanship, imbued with the invariable toughness and character of schooner men and their ships"-- Provided by publisher.
Identifiers: LCCN 2022039899 (print) | LCCN 2022039900 (ebook) | ISBN 9781948494618 (paperback) | ISBN 9781948494625 (epub)
Subjects: LCSH: Boudreau, R. L. (Robert Louis) | Seafaring life. | Schooners. | Ship captains--Canada--Biography. | Charter boat captains--West Indies--Biography.
Classification: LCC G540 .B4977 2022 (print) | LCC G540 (ebook) | DDC 910.4/5--dc23/eng20221121
LC record available at https://lccn.loc.gov/2022039899
LC ebook record available at https://lccn.loc.gov/2022039900

UNDER THE TRADE WIND SKY

Caribbean Adventures and Other Tales of the Sea

Captain Lou Boudreau

SEAWORTHY PUBLICATIONS, INC. • MELBOURNE, FLORIDA

Contents

Treasure Island 1
Caribbean Living 7
De Teef Pullin Man 11
The Voyage - Part I 17
The Voyage - Part II 25
The Return 29
A Year Before the Mast 33
The Dory Man of Cape Sable Island 43
The Last Harpooner 49
HMS Diamond Rock 55
The Flying Fish 63
Alone on the Great Atlantic 67
The Reef 73
Pirates of the Caribbean 79
"Overboard" 87
Fishes Alive 91
"Racing the Big Ones" 95
A Voyage on the Schooner Janeen 99
The Giant Pink Snail 105
Bupa the Elephant 109
Cleopatra's Barge II 113
Venus of Dominica 116
Lordy Lardy 123
Salvage 129

The Stingray	133
Roaches in Paradise	137
Island Squall	143
Of Barracudas and Men	147
The Schooners Yankee, Doubloon, and Windbloweth	153
Mama d'Leau	158
Perfidious Albion	162
The Bulls of Tarragona	166
"The Ufo of Petit St. Vincent"	171
Rumors	175
"The Legend of the Sylvania"	181
Wreckers	189
Of Pirate's Gold	195
The Romance of the Sea	199
The Men on the Moon and the Secret Lagoons of Marigot Bay	205
Mystery of the sea	209
Operation Rum Bottle	213
Landfall at Aves, - Isle of Birds	220
The Call of the Sea	224
A True Canadian Hero	229
Fire at Sea	233
A Sea of Dreams	240
About the Author	242

Prologue

A Voyage of Memories

It all began in the Windward Isles of the Caribbean,. Islands of sea people, born to a rich legacy of schooners and sailors who loved and understood the ocean. But who can say what draws us to the sea? Why do we feel uplifted as we face the ocean? Perhaps it is the music carried to us by the wind and the waves. Perhaps it is the fact that life itself consists mainly of water. Or could it be something else? Could it be the beautiful form of a graceful schooner making her way Southward? Surely above all, man's heart is moved by the sights and sounds of a sailing ship at sea. The movement of her hull through the water must be the seaman's ballet, the sound of the wind filling her sails the sailor's aria, and the love that he feels for his ship is that of a man for a woman.

The years have passed like leaves on the wind and my life has been like a magical dream. I was blessed with a wonderful memory, and I now share my thoughts as I recall the wonders of the sailorman's world. I want to share these tales with any who would hear them.

I was born a child of the sea and in my mind the pictures of those years are clear and beautiful. The stars in the night sky above the sails of the tall ship running before the wind were a wonder to behold. The dawn would break and bring to life a beautiful blue ocean, and my innocent gaze over the windward rail brought the salt spray to my face.

As a child under sail, I saw the coastlines of many countries beginning in the place of my birth where the regal green pine trees rose from sandy shores to lovely, forested hills.

My voyages took me to the islands of the Caribbean, and they were beautiful. I knew them all well as I sailed amongst them on my father's schooners. The pristine beaches and beautiful coral reefs blended with clear transparent water are imprinted forever on my mind.

Like my father I grew up to be a man of the sea, lucky to sail on some of the finest and most beautiful sailing ships afloat, and I loved them.

And now as I sail towards the next chapter of my life's voyage, I am again recalling the blue seas and green hilled islands where my adventure began all those years ago.

So dear reader, cast off and sail with me now, as we embark on a voyage of memories. The tales shared here are of sailing vessels and their crews in search of adventure across the Caribbean and Atlantic.

Captain Lou Boudreau

The author on the stern of Caribee at Treasure Island.

TREASURE ISLAND
A legacy fulfilled

There are rumors of a pirate's horde hidden on Norman Island in the British Virgin Islands, but what follows is no rumor. A fifty-year sea voyage ended not long ago on Quaker Island, off Chester, Nova Scotia. It was a voyage of plunder spanning the oceans and pirate redoubts across the globe. So read on brave reader to my tale faithful and true.

Many have read that best loved high-seas adventure novel, *"Treasure Island"* by Robert Louis Stevenson, but few lived it as we did. Sixty years ago, my father began a family tradition by reading *"Treasure Island"* to us at a very young age. Stevenson's descriptions inspired in us images of high seas piracy that followed us into our dreams. There were visions of jewels and gold coins, a map with the black spot, a buccaneer's cutlass, and the isle of Dead Man's Chest.

My siblings and I grew up sailing the Spanish Main aboard the *Caribee*, a full-sized replica of the famous Baltimore clipper schooners. Her long sleek black hull sported a row of gun ports and beneath her bowsprit a golden-haired figurehead guided us on our voyages. But apart from Stevenson's prose, there was never a man who could better capture a child's rapt attention than my late father, Captain Walter Boudreau. It was he who began our family tradition of hunting for buried treasure that would bring joy and wonder to our family for generations to come.

For my parents, the 1950s were formative years in their burgeoning sailing cruise business, but for my siblings and I, we looked only towards the horizon where Stevenson's infamous Skeleton Island lurked.

But it was there on Norman Island, a small Caribbean Isle in the blue expanse of the Caribbean Sea, that my father set in motion a tradition which forged dreams of buried treasure for generations. There, where the white coral sands and coconut trees rose to brush the Trade

Winds as they drifted over green forests and mountains, the die was cast.

It all began when I was six. One day the *Caribee* dropped anchor off Norman Island in the British Virgin Islands. Following a month-long primer of Stevenson's "*Treasure Island*," I already had visions of pirates and treasure swirling round my head sufficient to drive a kid batty.

My father, who was always known as the captain, drew up an authentic-looking map with the treasure spot, skull, and crossbones. Then under the cover of darkness he sent the crew of the 120-foot schooner *Caribee* ashore to hide the treasure and lay out the clues. An old wooden cigar box (funny how those old cigar boxes come in handy) filled with fake jewelry, copper pennies, and old coins of the Spanish Main. Pieces of driftwood, old shells, coconuts, fish bones, and odd bits of flotsam and jetsam that had washed up on the beach completed the fix.

At dawn, we rowed ashore and landed on the small, deserted beach at Treasure Point.

"Now, according to the map the treasure must be near the end of the beach, just by those rocks." the captain told me.

My gaze followed his arm towards the north end of the beach towards some loose rocks and bits of driftwood.

"Do you really think so, Daddy?" I asked excitedly.

"Oh, yes. See, the map says so." the captain replied, pointing to the black spot on the map.

It was a set-up like no other.

After a short hunt, I saw the corner of the old cigar box protruding from the sand and with shrieks of absolute joy, I held the box up for all to see.

Later, back aboard ship, I shared the booty as was the custom, each member of our pirate crew receiving a copper penny or shining bauble.

And so, in 1957 I found my first treasure. Today, I can still feel the excitement as I stood there with the treasure box in my hand. And to this day I still have the old West Indian copper coin.

Ever since that first treasure hunt, generations of little Boudreau's have pillaged and plundered beaches and shores worldwide in search of buried treasure. They would all succumb to the intrigue and mystique of *"Treasure Island"* and set out on adventures searching for buccaneer booty.

The Boudreau family later made a 14,000-mile voyage across the oceans aboard *Caribee* before she was sold to Twentieth Century Fox to make the movie "*A High Wind in Jamaica*," starring James Coburn and Anthony Quinn.

I married late in life to a lovely lass from the Isles of Scilly. After a few years of sailing the oceans together, we came to Canada and found a wonderful place to call home in the delightful village of Chester. We were then blessed with our own two children, Jason and Hannah. A few years later, our two young adventurers were ready to find their own treasure on the shores of Quaker Island.

Prior to our summer island visits, I began reading to Jason and Hannah some passages from *"Treasure Island*," preparing them for the treasure hunting season.

The day arrived and the time was at hand. The night before, as they sat sleepily on the sofa, I said "You know, I found this old treasure map in a cave about a year ago."

"A real treasure map?"

And then, as if that magical word suddenly registered in their brains, they jumped wide awake and hovered over the map. I played it down, but artfully dropped a few hints and waited to see if either one of them would bite.

"Look here," I said, pointing to the map, "There's a big, long beach with big rocks. It's probably nothing."

"A sandy beach? With big rocks Dad! We saw one yesterday. Do you think it could be the same one?" Jason pointed to the end of the map.

Hooked. Sarah and I knew neither one of them would sleep that night.

We went to wake the kids at dawn, but Jason and Hannah were up before sunrise, clutching their crumpled treasure maps in tight little fists while searching the house and yard for signs of Blackbeard. Their eyes were filled with wanderlust.

As we untied from the dock, Jason asked. "Dad, where's your pistol?"

"Oh, I've got it hidden."

I dodged that one.

The trip to Quaker Island on our 22-foot outboard powered pirate ship was short and before long we were standing on the shore walking down the beach. Jason and Hannah's excitement was palpable, but it was tempered by visions of Ben Gun, cutlasses, and Long John Silver hiding in the bushes by the beach.

"Now, we'll wait here while you go and find the treasure." I said.

"Is it safe to go?" Jason asked,

"Yes, don't worry, we'll be right here."

I mused momentarily as to what exactly I could do with a cutlass against Long John Silver.

The kids looked towards the loose pile of rocks to the north and then nervously began searching in earnest around the pieces of driftwood, jumping back with a start as a hermit crab lumbered away. So fevered was their hunt, they almost missed what they had come to find. But in a sandy spot behind a short bush, half buried in the white sand was an old wooden box.

Kneeling, Jason struggled with the latch, and then it popped open, exposing the contents to the brilliant sunlight. He ran his hands through the glittering pile of jewels, rings, and coins from across the Caribbean. A pirate's treasure for sure!

Sarah-Jayne and I heard their shrieks of joy and smiled.

"We found it! We found the treasure!" Jason screamed.

They were as happy then as they had ever been. And so, our lifelong search for treasure came full circle. As I looked into our children's eyes, I realized that the excitement they were feeling was certainly linked to a moment fifty years ago on a faraway West Indian isle.

But our real treasures were not found on old marine charts or cigar boxes filled with sparkling baubles. They were not found on deserted beaches and little-known cays on far away tropical islands, or beautiful pine treed isles on the coast of fair Nova Scotia. The real treasures are found in the eyes of children. That spark of youthful adventure which once ignited will burn forever.

The wanderlust has not faded with the passing of time. If anything, the arrival of our two children, Jason and Hannah, has re-ignited the old flame. We know not whom the next Boudreau Buccaneer will be, but of one thing we're sure.

"The treasure is there."

Lou, Pete, and Brian on deck in Longboat

CARIBBEAN LIVING

*I*twas in 1957, and one of my earliest memories was as a six-year-old boy sailing the Caribbean aboard the schooner *Caribee*, one of my father's sailing ships. My parents were pioneers of the windjammer passenger cruise business in the islands and I was living the childhood of dreams. The sights and sounds of the Windward Isles where I grew up are firmly etched upon my mind. Tall green mountainous islands formed a loose chain from South America in the south, to Puerto Rico in the north. Fine natural harbors and bays abounded where ships and boats of all sizes and shapes came and went on their business.

One of my first adventures took place when I found a small wooden chest of jewels and coins on Norman Island, Robert Louis Stevenson's actual *"Treasure Island."* Never mind that the treasure was planted for me or that the bandana wearing Benn Gun character coming out from the trees was one of our schooner's crew, it was real enough for me. The collection of coins and a few pieces of jewelry, though not a king's ransom, was a true and real treasure. During the months that followed, the old copper pieces shone as I counted them over and over, before returning them to the brass bound chest.

We sailed under trade wind skies across blue waters to beautiful islands where the coral reefs and white sand beaches beckoned. This book holds descriptions of life on a sailing ship as seen through the eyes of a young boy. Catching a blue marlin, visiting the famous Citadel in Haiti, and being kissed by Ava Gardner in Cuba, are only a few of my more vivid memories.

Our growing family settled in the enchanted lagoons of Marigot Bay, St Lucia, where we built a small hotel and marina called Yacht Haven Hotel (now Capella). The almost landlocked bay comprised an inner and outer lagoon, well-protected from the summer hurricanes by high surrounding mountains covered in rich green vegetation. It was hard to see from the sea, and unless you knew it was there you could easily miss it.

A beautiful sand spit lay to the north side of the bay covered with coconut trees. And then there was the inner lagoon. For me it was like some fairytale hideaway as indeed it was. Marigot Bay had a secret look. There was a tangible air of mystery on those calm waters, belying events and adventures long past that waited to be discovered again. Steep verdant hills rose all around, and the *Caribee* floated in crystal clear water. Green mangrove trees with spider like limbs covered in oysters descended into the clear water providing nurseries for small fish and not a few lobsters. Small red and yellow mangrove crabs wandered the roots while giant land crabs crawled the high tide mark. The bay was pristine, there was nothing there save what nature had put there. My siblings and I were fascinated by the lore of the island and became fluent in patois. Through cock fights and obeah our lives mirrored the rich tapestry of island life as it was then.

It was a different time. There was the dockside dentist who for a few BWI dollars pulled teeth with a pair of pliers after administering a swig of strong white rum. Our wonderful gardener, Simon, showed us how to eat the many wild fruits and vegetables that grew in profusion in the verdant valleys. We saw giant sperm whales harpooned by hand, to the lee of St. Vincent, and caught big sharks on the drop off. There were live volcanoes and a magical voyage to the mysterious lost atoll of Aves. The fabled isle is home to thousands of sea birds and abundant sea life and also the place where female sea turtles go to lay their eggs in the sand.

Sailing on my father's schooners through the islands, there were tales of storms and adventure on the high seas, as well as my perceptions of island, culture, and wonderful native people. It has been said by expats living in the islands that they were adopting their island homes. For us it was different. The people of St. Lucia adopted us and although our parents still thought of us as Canadian children, they were mistaken. We were truly children of the isles.

"*Where The Trade Winds Blow*" chronicles the life of a young boy experiencing the rich tapestry of island life of the era and the wonderful people who lived there. Swift schooners chart adventurous courses through the West Indies of the 1950s and later. Now, more than fifty years past, all I have left of my treasure is a British West Indian copper penny. Sometimes, as I sit by the fire on a cold winter evening, I take it and hold it in my hand. The copper grows warm and as I close my eyes, I see the *Caribee's* open quarterdeck. The brass cannon gleams and I see my treasure chest lying in the sand and feel the terror as Ben Gunn comes out from the edge of the trees.

A quote:

> "There resides in everyone the spirit of adventure, that small flame that inspires life's quest. All that is required is the kindling and then it will burn brightly The first sips of freedom's heavy brew are intoxicating and will pull you ever onwards, as it has me. Drink freely of it and you will not be disappointed. May fair winds fill your sails and the lee shore never find you"
>
> Capt. Robert Louis Boudreau

De Teef Pullin Man

De Teef Pullin Man

The sights and sounds of the Windward Islands where I grew up are firmly etched upon my mind. The tall mountainous islands formed a loose chain from South America in the south, to Puerto Rico in the north. Fine natural harbors and bays abounded where ships and boats of all sizes and shapes came and went on their business.

Port Castries, in St Lucia, was a bustling seaport in the sixties. A wonderful harbor on the western side of the island, it was well-protected from the northeast trade winds and big enough for the sailing craft of the day to tack into the harbor, if they needed to.

There were often a number of big former Nova Scotia fishing schooners in port. After a hard life on the Grand Banks of Newfoundland fishing cod, these magnificent vessels often ended their days as cargo carriers in the islands. Smaller, locally built schooners, based on their northern cousins came and went as well, busy with their missions of the day.

Two tall spars that frequented this port were those of my father's 138-foot steel Herreshoff charter schooner *Ramona*. She was the magic carpet that transported my siblings and I to the bays and hidden lagoons of the islands.

I have vivid memories of those hot balmy afternoons, when the white-hulled schooner lay alongside the Castries docks in St. Lucia.

There were no marinas in those days, and we would go there for provisioning, water, and fuel before leaving on a charter cruise. The docks were always a hive of activity, as the colorful characters that made a living on the wharf conducted their business. There was the professional rat catcher who put his struggling prey into a chicken wire cage before tossing it into the harbor to drown them. Muscular stevedores chanted and sang as they pushed their loads along the quay in big two wheeled carts. It was a busy port and the local trading schooners came and went, loading and unloading fish, oil drums, rum in barrels, cattle, and any other general cargo that was running between the islands. There was the self-important customs agent, whose favorite word was tomorrow, and further along, colorfully attired women in Madras headdresses hawked beads and straw hats to the tourists.

Then there was the "Teef Pullin Man." We had heard stories about the dentist who frequented the docks attending to the teeth of the local seamen, but we had never seen him. To us he remained a mysterious character whose basis in reality was tenuous at best. That was until one morning when I was about ten years old.

One day, as the *Ramona* lay alongside the Castries wharf with the water hose filling her tanks, my brother Peter, sister Janeen, and I were perched on the furled headsails out on the bowsprit monitoring the bustling activity on the shore. It was a good vantage point providing us excellent views of all that went on along the wharf.

As we watched, a peculiar looking fellow emerged from a small group near the town gate, which was very near to us. Short, with white curly hair, he wore a white shirt and frayed black suit. Small round spectacles perched on his nose and although he presented an almost comical caricature, the expression on his face was serious and confident, befitting the importance of his profession. Below his short trousers he sported a pair of lace up dress shoes which in keeping with the custom of the islands had been lovingly preserved with many layers of white paint.

"Look," I exclaimed in awe, "it's him, the Teef Pullin Man."

The little man paused for a moment to scan the waterfront as if assessing the number of prospective clients and then, with a purposeful air, he squared his shoulders and swaggered down the dock in our direction. In one hand he carried a black satchel containing the tools of his trade, and in the other a small wooden box. Passing our perch, he paused at the trading schooner moored just ahead of us to offer his services.

"Teef pullin, teef pullin, all you ain't have no teef to pull?" he called to the men working on the vessel's deck.

A strong looking seaman paused momentarily from his task on the stern. Looking towards the man on the shore he briefly rubbed his jaw. A moment later he vaulted the rail to the dock. After a brief consul-

DE TEEF PULLIN MAN

tation the dentist placed his wooden box down on the stone wharf near the schooner's stern.

"Sit dung heh an open you mouth." he ordered, and the seaman obeyed.

A swift preliminary examination ensued. The "Teef Pullin Man" unceremoniously bent the sailor's head back and proceeded to have a good look inside his mouth. Above the bustle of the dock noise, we heard his diagnosis.

"It rotten yes, got to come out." he announced.

The patient nodded resignedly and prepared himself for the operation. The "Teef Pullin Man" reached into his satchel pulling out a bottle of the liquid he used as anesthetic, handing it to the sailor man.

"Drink lil' bit o' dis." he instructed.

The burly seaman took more than a little bit, causing him to shake his head violently, A moment later the unmistakable sweet smell of high-octane Jack Iron white rum wafted over the bowsprit. Then it was down to business. Taking a large pair of rusty pliers from the black bag, the "Teef Pullin Man" held them away from his side and poured rum over the end.

"To disinfek," we heard him explain to the sailor.

The patient leaned his head back, opening his mouth as wide as he could.

The dentist made a quick sign of the cross and then with great purpose went in with the pliers. In our eagerness to watch, my sister almost fell from her perch into the dirty harbor, but the bowsprit net caught her before she got there.

"Is he doing it?" she asked unable to watch.

"Yes, look quick. He's doing it to him with the big pliers." I replied helpfully.

My sister covered her eyes.

The poor seaman began to struggle, but despite his diminutive stature, the "Teef Pullin Man" was very strong, and putting an arm around the sailor's throat he continued. A small crowd had gathered around by then and they all had advice to offer.

"Give de po man some mo rum nuh, you can't see him in pain?" the rat catcher said.

"But wait, you pullin de wrong toof you know." said a stevedore.

The captain of the trading schooner came ashore to sort things out and took hold of the seaman's shoulders from behind, helping to hold him still.

"What you waitin' for nuh? Pull de damn toof out." he urged the dentist.

The pot-bellied cook from the schooner had come ashore too, and he stood by in his soiled apron waving his arms above his head.

"All you ain't know what de hell you doin, you got to give de man a good blow in de back of he head for de toof to come out." he shouted excitedly.

At that point, several swarthy-faced fellows volunteered to do the job, but the "Teef Pullin Man" staved them off with his pliers and the merciless surgery continued.

I held my breath as the dentist worked his elbow vigorously back and forth and then suddenly, the little crowd surrounding the seaman erupted in a loud applause.

"Look de toof, de toof, it out, it out." they chanted.

The "Teef Pullin Man's" hand flew triumphantly upwards brandishing an impossibly large tooth held in the jaws of the plies. He flourished it above his head like a prize for all to see before tossing it into the harbor in front of us, where it fell with a tiny plop. The seaman availed himself of another ample shot of the Jack Iron, and after paying the three dollars, climbed unsteadily back aboard the schooner to resume his work.

Washing his pliers in the harbor in front of the *Ramona's* bowsprit, he noticed us for the first time and smiled.

"Hello chilrens, all you ain't have any toof-aches?" He asked smiling.

Terror stricken we began edging towards the bow of the schooner.

"No, our teefs is good, real good." I replied shaking my head.

"Yes, we brushes them every day." my sister added nodding.

"Wif toot paste," my little six-year-old brother assured him smiling.

"Ah, very good then, perhaps a nudder time."

We hoped not.

Bidding us goodbye, he squared his shoulders and moved off in the direction of the next trading schooner calling out the chant of his trade.

"Teef Pullin, teef pullin, all you ain't have no teef to pull?"

None of us would ever again dispute the existence of the "Teef Pullin Man."

Ramona heads north to Nova Scotia.

The Voyage – Part I

Pennant Cove

Fifty years ago, I was a 16-year-old deckhand on my father's schooner *Ramona* on a voyage from the West Indies to Lunenburg. We had been at sea for a month or so on passage from the island of St. Lucia and the 138-foot schooner was scheduled to berth at the Lunenburg Foundry and Smith & Rhuland shipyards for a refit that summer. We were twelve aboard; my father the captain, brothers Peter and Brian, sister Janeen, mate Joel Dressel, and other crew.

The sailing in the lower latitudes of the Caribbean had been true to form. Passing close to the west of the windward and leeward islands and through the Virgin Islands, the northeast trade winds carried us up and on through the Bahamas. After a stop in Miami for fuel and provisions we joined the great Gulf Stream for the trip north along the coast of the USA. It was here that we ran into a storm.

Off the Virginia Capes, we encountered gale force winds and high seas.

"We have to heave to" my father told us.

We struck the jib, foresail, and main, and hove to with the storm trysail. The trysail was a very heavy strong sail that was made for heavy weather. The jumbo was always of heavier canvas or Dacron and had more tabling and reinforcements built into it because it was the sail that was flown till last.

The gale passed and a day or so later we found ourselves becalmed on the outer reaches of Georges Bank. This huge underwater plateau can precipitate some of the oceans worst weather, but on this day the great Atlantic was calm. Not a ripple broke the surface and we proceeded to lower away the main and headsails, leaving the foresail to steady her. The big diesel coughed to life as we motored slowly northwards at about seven knots. As we left the main part of the Gulf Stream the weather turned chillier. We were well over Georges then and my father slowed to take a sounding. Smiling he turned to the crew.

"Get your lines out boys he said there's fish below us for sure." he said.

We prepared some heavy colored jigs and dropped them to the bottom. As the schooner drifted, we lowered our lines and soon the whole crew was jigging off the bottom. As I pulled the jig up and down, I suddenly felt a heavy weight on my line. I pulled hard and the fish came slowly upwards.

"What kind of fish is this" I asked as I pulled a 20-pound fish over the rail?

A grey brown color with thick lips, I had certainly never seen one before.

"That's a codfish." my father replied smiling.

Later, with a pile of cod on deck we hauled in our lines and sailed slowly northwards in a light breeze towards the coast of Nova Scotia. As we sailed towards our destination of Lunenburg, a heavy fog rolled in. Our radar was broken, and because we hadn't seen the sun to take a sextant sight for several days, the captain had been running on dead reckoning alone.

We were suddenly lost on a dangerous coast, but there were other seafarers there hidden in the fog and the tradition of mariners offering help to one another on the high seas would soon come into play.

The very light breeze held as we slowly closed the coast, but the fog didn't lift. It was eerie as wisps flowed gently around the schooner's deck like ethereal beings. Our masts disappeared above us as it wafted gently across the sails. After a while, the wind died away and the sea became calm and still. We lowered the sails and then the only sound was the muffled belching of the main engine as it pushed us slowly along.

The captain began to grow worried. We had run down our distance and still saw no land. He estimated that we should be near our destination of Lunenburg, but there was no sign of it. Only the dense fog. We had three lookouts then, one aloft in the foremast cross trees and one on each bow. There was a tenseness on the *Ramona's* deck as all hands strained to see through the mist. Suddenly, we heard the mournful cry of the foghorn and the captain reduced speed so that we were barely coasting through the water. Joseph stood by forward with the lead line to take soundings. We tried to hone in on the fog signal because the captain and Joel felt that it was a buoy and not a ship and eventually it emerged from the fog just ahead of us. My father, for want of a better plan, decided to tie up. We quickly launched the longboat and Louis and I pulled over to the buoy with a bow line from the schooner and made it fast.

"Not exactly legal," the captain said, "But under the circumstances we'll do it."

We swung to the buoy while the captain looked at the chart. I could see that he was tense. The number on the buoy indicated that we were tied up to the Pennant Cove marker several miles south of Halifax, but the area looked most perilous with numerous underwater rocks and ledges. The current had taken us much faster than we thought, and we had overrun our destination by a fair margin.

It wasn't long before a white hulled Cape Island lobster boat appeared out of the fog with two fishermen aboard.

"Ahoy," they called.

"Ahoy to you." the captain replied, and the lobster boat came alongside.

They were Melvin Gray and Charlie Marryatt from Pennant Cove. They had returned from their nets to find us tied to the Seaway Buoy.

"Where you from?" they asked.

"We're from the West Indies bound for Lunenburg." the captain replied.

"Well, you're a bit north of there." Melvin said.

"We need a safe place to anchor until this fog clears." our captain said. "Can you help us?"

Melvin didn't hesitate.

"I'll take you into Pennant Cove, skipper." Melvin said, "just cast off the buoy there and follow me. I'll put Charlie here aboard to stand on the bow." Melvin instructed.

There followed an amazing feat of seamanship. Melvin's Cape Island lobster boat took up station fifty feet ahead of the *Ramona's* bowsprit and we cast off the buoy.

We followed slowly as Melvin's boat drifted in and out of the fog like a ghost while Charlie stood on our bow relaying directions aft.

"Come to port just a little."

"That's it now, starboard two spokes."

"Steady as she goes, hold her just like that."

These directions were relayed from Melvin to Charlie on the bow of the schooner and aft to the captain at the wheel and he steered us through the thick fog. We could see nothing, but after a while we heard the sounds of seas breaking on rocks. After about forty-five minutes the lobster boat slowed right down.

"Get your anchor ready now." the word came back.

All was quiet on the deck of the *Ramona* now. No one knew where we were and we still couldn't see a thing, but there was a difference now. The surface of the water was truly calm, the type of calm found only in sheltered water. The ocean had ceased to roll, and the schooner *Ramona* sat solidly in the water decks moving not at all.

"Sounding" the captain called forward.

Joseph started swinging the lead line and when he had a good arc, he let lead fly forward. It splashed into the water thirty feet ahead of where he stood at the rail just forward of the starboard rigging.

"By the mark five," he called back.

"By the mark four."

"Stop your engines and standby." Charlie called aft.

"You can let her go now skipper." Melvin shouted back from the lobster boat under the bow.

THE VOYAGE – PART I

After a signal from the captain, the mate swung a hammer at the pin holding the heavy fishermen anchor on the davit and with a big splash it fell to the water. We looked around, there was still nothing to be seen just the quiet stillness and the thick fog. There was a strange aura about. There was an earthy smell, and I caught the scent of pine trees and salt cod, but for all of that there was no indication that we were anchored anywhere other than on the high seas.

The lobster boat came alongside, and Melvin climbed aboard.

"How do you think were laying" asked the captain.

"Oh, good enough, you give her a bit more chain and you should be just fine." Melvin said.

Our crew went to their bunks tired, but relieved. When dawn broke the next morning, the fog had cleared. We were in tiny Pennant Cove and there was not room there for another large vessel to anchor. Melvin and Charlie, with the knowledge of a lifetime's fishing off the Cove, had brought us through the thickest fog without hesitation. There was only a small opening lined with jagged rocks on either side and ahead of us a tiny fishing village and astern a promontory with pine trees. It was indeed a daunting feeling to look at the opening through which we had come and to realize that we had done so blind.

A day later, we made the short passage to Lunenburg and all hands were on deck as the schooner came into the picturesque fishing port. I stood in the forward rigging, along with Pete in yellow slickers, as we approached the dock at the Lunenburg Foundry. The engine room telegraph jangled and the heaving line snaked ashore. We came alongside the dock and the long voyage north was over.

Some years ago, I returned to Pennant Cove. I wanted to find the men whose great seamanship came to our aid all those years ago, but I was doubtful. Forty years is a long time. My wife Sarah-Jayne and I wandered the Pennant area looking for anyone who might remember the *Ramona*. I talked to a number of folks, but no one was old enough to remember. Finally, we met a fisherman who thought he might know who it was that delivered us from peril decades before.

He took us to the home of Melvin Gray. He was then still a fit looking man with a ready smile and the unmistakably sharp eyes of a lifelong seafarer. I asked him if he was the one who helped the schooner that was in trouble here 1967. I said that some fishermen had guided us to safety.

And then I showed him the photograph of the *Ramona*. He squinted at the picture for only a moment and his face lit up. "That's her," he said "I remember her now. She was tied to the buoy and Charlie and I guided her in."

And so he had. We talked for a while about that day so many years before and I thanked him again for the kindness he'd shown us. I told him that we were very lucky to have had the benefit of his great seamanship that day. He said that the fog on that day was one of the thickest he could remember.

It was a good feeling to have met this man again after so many years. Sadly, Melvin is gone now and Charlie as well. And so was born another tale of the sea. Two great seamen of Pennant Cove are gone now, but the memory of what they did all those years ago remains. I remember them now and thank them again for their kindness and great seamanship.

Ramona showing her new three-masted rig at the shipyard dock in Lunenburg, Nova Scotia prior to departure for the West Indies.

The Voyage - Part II
Peril on the Sea

After arriving at the port of Lunenburg, we spent the summer there, where my father converted *Ramona* to a three-master. He added a third spar to break up her huge mainsail. She would be far easier to handle then. On the dry dock, her bad plates were cut out and new ones welded in. The old deck was removed, and new edge grain pine laid down.

My job for the summer was to supply the crew with fish. My parents had rented a small cottage in Mader's Brook, near Lunenburg and we kept the schooner's longboat there. I used to leave in the morning with my dory, compass, and chart, headed to an area just to the south of Tancook Island. There I found haddock aplenty and some cod as well. We ate well from Nova Scotia's ocean bounty that summer. I found thick fogs at times, but my compass always led me northwest back to the land. I can remember at age 16, my father trying to see if I wanted to get a driver's license. I declined. What use were such things? The Great Atlantic, my longboat, and the dories were far more important to me.

It was often said that the men who sailed schooners to the Grand Banks to fish from dories were some of the best. The two-man dories were launched from the mother ships and longlines for cod were set. They later rowed or sailed back to unload their catch and their dories were hoisted aboard to be stowed on deck.

This was a most perilous occupation and many fine men never returned to their waiting schooners. Dory men were lost and swallowed by the sea never to be found.

Lewis and I were fellow deckhands on the *Ramona* and we had sailed and rowed the *Ramona's* longboat and fished in the islands of the West Indies. Even at age 16 we were strong young men. We were like brothers, he and I, and now we would be dory mates, friends for life. My friend Lewis and I decided that we would row in the dory races that year. It was an historical event in the famed town of Lunenburg.

We practiced our rowing around the course and my father's smile as we bent to the oars was a fine thing to see. On the day of the race, Lewis and I rowed our two-man banks dory to the starting line and put our stern to the rope. When the gun fired, we bent the oars and took off. At first, we seemed to hold our own, but as we raced down the course another dory took the lead. As hard as we rowed, we could not hold them, and we ended up second. My father was happy, and Lewis and I were applauded on our second-place win.

Who could have known that two young boys growing up in a secluded lagoon in the West Indies would row in these famed races? Our relationship was firm, and we were like brothers and dory mates.

At the end of the refit, the *Ramona* left Lunenburg under the command of Captain Ross McKay, a respected Master Mariner with a good record of experience under sail. Despite my protestation, I was ordered back to school in Barbados. Lewis would sail on the *Ramona*.

My father could not bring the ship south himself because he was needed at the hotel in Marigot Bay in St. Lucia. So, Ross McKay was engaged to deliver the ship to the Islands, where my father would take command again.

The *Ramona* sailed in December 1967 with a full crew including the West Indians who had sailed her north and several Canadians. The voyage began well enough. The schooner excelled under her new rig, but trouble began when they ran into a very bad winter storm northeast of Bermuda. The *Ramona* took a terrible beating and most of her sails blew out. However, she was a strong ship and was never in any danger of foundering.

During the storm, the *Ramona* drifted closer to Bermuda's deadly shoals, and she eventually took the reef seven miles to the northeast of Bermuda. Lying on her side in the coral beds, she was pounded by the huge surf. My friend Lewis and four of the other crew left in the dories and tried to get ashore. They could see the lights, but they were deceptive. At night, they seemed to be much closer than they really were, and they drowned in the surf.

It was during this term that the headmaster of my school called me and gave me the news that the *Ramona* had been wrecked in Bermuda

THE VOYAGE – PART II

with loss of life. I came home from school a few days later with a dismal report card and the excuse from Commander Wilkes that I was disturbed because of the wreck and that because of that I was unable to apply myself to my work. Well, he was right. All I could think about was the *Ramona* being pounded on the reef and my friend and dory mate Lewis drowning in the surf.

This disaster weighed heavily on my mind. The fact that I had been the one who petitioned my father to give my friend Lewis the job on *Ramona* made me feel at least partially responsible for his death. That was a heavy load for a sixteen-year-old to bear and for many months, I felt a terrible heaviness in my heart that would not go away.

My father was also devastated. Seamen in his employ had perished and he had lost his schooner. I felt at the time that I had an insight as to how he felt and sometimes in the evenings I would watch him as he sat on the dock in Marigot and stared out at the harbor with a hurt look in his eyes.

My friend Lewis and the others who perished were laid to rest in the seaman's cemetery of Bermuda, and the survivors went to their places of origin. A group of Bermudans later salvaged the *Ramona*, but when she was finally floated, they found that her once proud hull was twisted beyond repair. It was a terrible waste of good young lives and a sad end to a fine ship.

*Ramona after salvage in Bermuda.
Sadly, She was later sunk as a dive reef*

THE RETURN

The following year I came to a decision. I would go to sea. When I told my parents that I would no longer be returning to the school they accepted this perhaps a bit resignedly. They had known all along that I would be a sea wanderer.

"OK Lou, if that's what you really want, but no sitting around home here. If you want to go to sea, then that's what you'll do." my father said.

Within a month I was fortunate to join the famous schooner *Bluenose II* as a deckhand and thus officially began my life on the ocean. After discharging our passengers, the *Bluenose II* left St. Lucia bound for Lunenburg, Nova Scotia. We set the four lowers and laid our course to the north. The smells of the land faded and now there was just the sea. The odor of lush green tropical mountains, trees and damp earth was gone, replaced by the crisp aroma of the deep blue ocean.

We left the world of mortal men behind us, transcending into that of the north Atlantic schooner man. Far from land, our speeding schooner rolled gently, dipping her lee rail before surging on. The *Bluenose II* was in her element; a white winged sea spirit dancing to a tune only the sailor man knows. The ocean catches her lee deadeyes in a rush of spray before she lifts, and above her decks tall spars carry a press of taught canvas. Well-trimmed jibs and foresail pull her onwards even as the main and topsails push her ever faster. Stays, sheets and halyards strain to hold their willful charges and as I tilt my head slightly, I can hear her wooden spars moan and laugh in the language of the deep-sea schooner. Occasionally, when she takes a deep roll, the end of her long main boom tastes the sea, rending it with a quickly healing wound. Her long black hull leaves a frothy wake astern, even as her perfect symmetry of sail glides serenely above the turbulent ocean like some graceful white winged seabird.

In the morning sunlight, the droplets of ocean coming over the rail glisten like so many flying diamonds before reaching my face. The feel of the salt spray is invigorating, and as I lick the salt from around my mouth, I savour the taste. We seem almost inconsequential on the empty expanse of the great ocean and as I scan the horizon, we appear to be alone. But we are not. Sea birds accompany us on our way; small dark petrels dive and disappear between the troughs of the waves, fluttering madly to keep up with us. They seem happy, almost playful, and not in the least concerned about their seemingly isolated location.

The deep-sea routine is traditional and time honored. Three squares a day and while the fare is simple the crew wolf it down without complaint. The schooner needs constant care, and we attend to our duties as the hours pass. The mate adds another piece of baggywrinkle to the foremast aft lower shroud and the bosun cobbles up a start in the jumbo clew before it opens further. We stand our wheel watches trying our best to keep the fast-moving vessel on her course. Inevitably someone strays and the mate is there in a second.

"Keep her steady, there" he growls.

The skipper raises his sextant at noon and by some method known only to him he places our latitude. He checks the rig and trim every watch and if need be he orders a pull here or a foot slacked off there.

Evening comes on the *Bluenose II* and the ship's bell rings in the turn of the watch. As the sun sinks in the west a cloak of darkness covers the schooner, but she rolls on, uncaring of the change. For her, the ocean remains infinite, and her purpose on it unchanged. For us, however, there is magic; the aura of the ocean night casts a spell on the schooner that is very special. The eerie glows of the port and starboard lights throw ghostly color into the salt spray as it rises from the bow. Like an endless kaleidoscope show, sudden flashes of red, then green, then darkness again. Just forward of the wheel the red tinted binnacle light turns the helmsman's face into a bizarre demon-like visage and the glow of the lookout's cigarette stands out like a tiny red beacon in the night. The schooner feels more alive than ever during the hours of darkness. Perhaps because we can no longer see her, we more consciously feel her. She lifts her stem gently, reaping the night wind and then heeling slightly, she takes sustenance from it before rolling on. Under the lee bow a wave of white water rises, higher even than the rail, but as the schooner surges forward, it curves away to fall on the dark Atlantic, rolling away to leeward with an angry hiss. White water races away from the lee rail in almost magical form before disappearing into nothingness. The zone of blackness ends as I glance aloft. There, the tips of her topmasts trace a meandering course through an endless sea of stars.

On our voyage north to Nova Scotia on the *Bluenose II*, we stopped in St. Georges, Bermuda. I knew that the hulk of the *Ramona* had been raised and I resolved to go and see her. Capt. Coggins, a seaman of great knowledge, perhaps understood what lay before me and instructed that none should accompany me, that this was something I must do alone. A taxi took me to Hamilton dockyard where her hull was tied up. I wandered her twisted decks and went below. I saw the ghosts then, my dory mate Lewis and others. I saw the faces of my ship mates who had crossed the bar and the voices of our crew setting sail. After a few moments I returned to the deck and sat on the aft hatch.

And so, it came to pass. A young sailor man 17 years old sat on the deck of the raised wreck of the *Ramona* looking out past the sea buoy to the Atlantic. A few passersby stopped, perhaps sensing a profound moment. They could not know. My dory mate was gone, swallowed by the cruel sea and never more to row with me a dory again.

Later my taxi took me to the seaman's graveyard, and I knelt at the stone where the men of the *Ramona's* names were scribed. I left a small piece of paper there that held a short message that none will ever see. None but my dory mate, Lewis.

A seventeen-year-old deckhand serves aboard the famed Bluenose II.

A Year Before the Mast

A Voyage in the Schooner Bluenose II

Gazing out over the ocean I take a deep breath. A low fog bank hovers just beyond the Mahone Bay islands, a tangible, if not impenetrable barrier between the land and the blue sea beyond. There is magic here and sometimes on days like this as I look out over the bay, I imagine the ghost of a tall Atlantic schooner racing across the ocean. I see her topmasts bending under a press of sail and hear the whistle of the wind in her rigging. Her huge white bow wave rolls gracefully away to leeward, and I can almost hear the creak of block and tackle.

But it is no dream or fancy of my imagination; it is a memory. Looking over to the mantelpiece where the wooden ship model sits, it all comes back to me. The three-foot reproduction of the great schooner is a link to my past and she stirs powerful yearnings in my heart. I built her over a period of years, carefully, and without haste, a labor of love. The recollection is warm and comfortable, the hours sitting at my desk in the study pinning small basswood planks to their frames, rigging a backstay aft and a jib halyard forward. Building her from scratch, with only my memory as a guide, the hull had emerged from the hundreds of small wood strips as if by magic, my big hands almost instinctively knowing how to shape her. Perhaps this was because I knew her so well, but it had not always been so. There was a time all those years ago when it had truly been only a dream. I was but a youth when I went to sea in her, a young man following his heart to sail across the oceans in search of adventure. It had been a time of great awakenings, when like an open ledger, the pages of my mind were filled and what was written then has had much to do with what has since come to pass.

Taking the old leather-bound journal from the side table, I run my hand over the cover. Although almost fifty years have passed, the name "*Bluenose II*" is still there.

Smiling slightly, I close my eyes and the result is inevitable. As if caught in a time warp, the years roll back, and I am standing on her deck again. I am struggling to hold the big schooner to her northerly course and my hands are beginning to cramp. The pressure of the big wheel's thick spokes has molded my palms into two almost paralytic claws and even though I've only been on the helm for forty minutes of my scheduled two-hour wheel watch, it seems like an eternity. We are on the starboard tack under storm trysail, foresail, and headsails beneath an ever-darkening sky and as another of the strengthening gusts hit us the big wooden schooner's 143-foot hull heels over until her varnished cap rail disappears under the white water rushing down her lee side. The big brass compass port that we polished so religiously over the past months is now green streaked and coated with north Atlantic salt, and looking inside, I catch the lubber line moving almost imperceptibly to the west. Handing a couple of spokes to port, I haul her down again. The skipper is standing as he always does just to windward and forward of the helm position, legs spread with feet planted firmly on the deck to brace against the roll. He purses his lips slightly; am I handling her right?

Opening my eyes again, I have a yearning for more. The pages are well worn, and I finger them carefully as they will be opened again whenever I feel the need. Reading from the beginning I relive the day I joined the *Bluenose II* and the voyage of 1968. At age 17, I joined the ship in Marigot Bay, St. Lucia where my father ran his schooner cruise business.

We sailed the following day. After boarding our new passengers at about ten, we heaved anchor bound for a group of islands to the south known as the Tobago Cays. Under the able command of Captain Ellsworth T. Coggins, the big schooner spread her white wings and on a southerly course reaped a good northeast trade wind, just off the quarter.

The *Bluenose II* was a fine vessel, and I soon began to feel pride in my ship. Whenever her tall spars glided gracefully into the harbor, people lined the shore to admire her long sleek hull. They must have felt the same sense of awe that I did, remembering a time when her namesake was the best and fastest in the world. Ahead, the open sea is waiting for us. But before getting sail on, there are many tasks that we need to take care of and we go about stowing the dock lines, fenders, and the like in their places. No orders are necessary; we know what to do.

We've come about a mile out but the skipper's looking to get a little more sea room to make sail as we get ready for the hoist. There's very little motion on the schooner's deck and the sea is smooth.

We check that the two ships launches are sitting securely in their chocks and lashed properly to the big pad eyes in the deck. Each boat has a canvas cover, which we check and snug down.

The big 300-pound port and starboard fisherman anchors lay catted on the rail on either side of the anchor windlass. They're lashed to the catheads and to eyebolts in the deck. They need to be well-secured. If we run into heavy seas, we want to make sure they don't shift at all. The port and starboard chains that run from the anchor shackles to the hawse pipes and into the ship are pulled tight so that they can't swing around. Then first mate Skodje has us lash some old canvas around each chain so they can't damage the hull paintwork. We stuff "puddings" in the holes where the chains lead from the deck down to the chain locker. In a heavy sea water will find its way below any way it can. Sods law again.

We've motored out from the land a way now, at least one mile, and the skipper thinks we've got enough sea room to make sail. As the schooner begins to turn slowly into the wind, Skodje goes below.

"All hands on deck to make sail." he shouts.

The crew are expecting the call and come up immediately.

The skipper orders slow ahead, and the *Bluenose* slows, coming dead into the wind. The skipper will carefully hold her there as we go about the hoist.

The main goes up first. The throat and peak halyards are run through fairleads on each side of the deck to the big hydraulic anchor winch drums forward. The chain clutches have been disengaged and the winch can now be used for hoisting sail. Dave and Rosemond tail the halyards while Craig works the winch control. I tend the main peak down haul. It's in a coil on the deck and I must make sure that it doesn't foul as it goes up. The mate stands at the main tabernacle making sure that nothing goes wrong. Mike tends the peak guy holding the gaff from swinging too much. I stand aft by the main sheet and quarter tackles. We've rendered a few feet of slack into the main sheet, the toping lifts, and end lift raised so that the boom now sits a good foot above the gallows frame. Skodje will watch the topsail sheet, which must be rendered as the sail goes up.

The skipper gives Skodje the thumbs up and he signals the winch to start hoisting. The two halyards come tight, and the sail slowly begins to climb the mast. The *Bluenose* is awakening. She had been asleep before, but now her spirit stirs. The creaking of the blocks and the sounds of the sail going up are signals that soon she will be about that for which she was built. She shudders slightly, anticipating the moment when her wings will fill with the freshening breeze.

The big four thousand eight hundred square foot sail continues slowly up the mast. The sail hoops slide easily on the spar. They have been well-greased and don't stick at all. Mike tweaks the peak guy line for a moment, making sure that the gaff goes up cleanly between the two topping lifts. Sometimes, if she is rolling heavily, he will have trouble with this, but today it is easy; the sea is relatively smooth in the lee of St. Lucia. He also guides the gaff to the starboard side of the end lift; we will be on the port tack. The skipper diligently keeps the schooner into the wind, if she falls off too much the mainsail will bind on the rigging and the crew will have to stop hoisting until he brings her back. But he keeps her dead on. The throat reaches the top of its hoist and Skodje gives the signal to stop the winch.

The main throat halyard needs to be made fast on the belaying pin in the tabernacle but there is far too much strain on the line for the crew to shift it, if the man on the winch were to slack, it would just lower the sail back down. This is the mate's job. Skodje puts a rolling hitch into the halyard using the heavy line spliced to the eyebolt of the halyard block on the deck. He holds it in place while nodding foreword towards Craig on the starboard winch drum. He eases back slowly, letting Skodje's rolling hitch gradually take the strain. As soon as the full load is held by the hitch, he whips off the halyard, allowing Dave enough slack to make it fast. The halyard has been transferred from the winch to the belaying pin. Skodje signals for the peak halyard on the opposite side to continue up and the winch starts again. Soon the peak reaches the top of its hoist, and the skipper lets the *Bluenose* come to starboard just a degree or two. She will be on the port tack and he's putting just enough wind in the sail to stop it from flogging but not enough to hamper its final hoist. Neil the bosun puts some slack into the lee topping lifts now so that they don't hamper the sail as it fills to starboard.

"Take off the lazy quarter tackle now." the skipper says.

The peak is almost all the way up now.

"You can take off the other one now and go ahead and put six feet of slack into the sheet."

We watch as Skodje and Mike put the final tension on the peak and throat halyards using the halyard purchases. The gaff rigged sail, for it to set the way it should, must be peaked up properly. If it isn't brought up well enough the sail will set baggy and sag. Skodje brings her up good and tight.

The schooner falls off a little to starboard now, just enough to fill the aft third of the mainsail. The halyards have been made fast and the sheet is fine for the moment.

We move to the foresail now and it's hoisted the same way as the main. Throat and peak halyards run to the winch and the toping lifts are tended the same as the main. It is peaked up properly and the halyards made fast on the forward pin rail. Skodje holds with the rolling hitches while the deckhands shift the halyards from the winch to the belaying pins. We handle the downhaul, guy, and topsail sheet the same way we did on the main. No different. Skodje sheets it out the same extent as the main and the skipper lets the Bluenose come a little more to starboard now, filling the main and foresail.

Next comes the jumbo. Once more it's thumbs up and we crew go to it. There's a special rhythm for hauling the easier halyards by hand and we begin a chant.

"One two, one two, one two."

One man can't hoist the sail: it's much too heavy. Even for two it's hard and a third usually joins in at the top of the hoist. But can you imagine six arms flying up and down trying to grab a line and pull it down in unison? There's a method to the hoist that's like a well-rehearsed dance. Usually, two men of differing height start out. The shorter man always places his hand just below the taller man's. This way every time the chant calls for him to place his hand on the rope it goes below the other man's hand, and all goes smoothly. When the third joins he takes the last or lowest hand position. The jumbo goes up quickly and Skodje trims it roughly to suit the other two sails. When it's at the top of the hoist, he slacks the topping lift. It was holding the boom up too high causing the sail to sag. But it's okay now, forming a beautiful curve. They take the final inches on the halyard using the jumbo jig and the sail is well set, with no scallops on the hoist.

Of all the sounds on our schooner, the creaking of the blocks, the gurgling sound of the sea as it runs aft along the lee rail; the sounds of the big, galvanized hanks whizzing up the head stays are most like music to my ears. A good pair on the halyard, working well together hand over hand and chanting as they go.

'One, two, One two, One two."

"Whiz, whiz, whiz." Each time they pull it's schooner music.

Now we're ready for the jib. As it runs aloft the skipper spokes the wheel to leeward a bit. When the sail is at the top of its hoist, we sheet it in with the benefit of having no wind in it. The other sails aft and to windward have blanketed it.

The *Bluenose* is under what we call the four lowers, main, foresail, jib, and jumbo. The skipper brings her onto her course on the port tack and we go about trimming up for the slant. Our course puts the wind abeam and the sails need to be sheeted in or out to suit.

Meanwhile we're beginning to trim the sheets from aft. The big schooner is feeling the freshening breeze and I am excited. The mate goes to the big main sheet bit and slacks a few feet. There's a slight groove that the heavy line is even now making for itself in the new wood. The big sail and boom edge slowly out over the water. When he judges it to be right, he makes fast and moves to the foresails. Each sail is trimmed to the one aft of it, as well as to the wind. The foresail is backwinding the main now and we slack it out until it stops. As soon as the dimple in the leading edge of the mainsail disappears, we know that we've got it pretty close. The foresail boom is then set so that it is lying at an angle just slightly less than that of the main. Then on to the jumbo and finally the jib. When Skodje has trimmed the four lowers to his satisfaction, he comes aft again.

"How's that look Skipper?" he asks.

Captain Coggins looks forward for a moment, and then nods.

From our location at the stern of the schooner we can sight along the deck, and I see that the three booms, main, fore, and jumbo all line up together, with the angle decreasing only a few degrees or so going forward. And the jib's outer curve follows the shape of the others exactly. The sails are well trimmed for this course and the *Bluenose* comes alive.

The sky is blue with a few scudding white clouds and the wind increases to a good twenty knots. The sea is moderate, but as we leave the St. Lucia coast behind us the dark blue surface begins to undulate, and a gentle swell begins to roll in from the north. Our schooner feels it. She moves now, like a thing alive. The occasional dollop of warm Atlantic spray comes over the rail and flies aft. We laugh and wipe our faces, licking the salty brine from our lips. It is a good taste. I begin to feel that special feeling that only a sailing man knows. We're part of our *Bluenose* and she's part of us. She's giving us our reward now. She can't do what she's doing without our help and now she'll dance for us. After a half hour the wind is still steady and just abaft of the beam.

Skodje returns to the helm. He's made a round of the decks carefully making sure everything is shipshape.

The skipper puts Neil on the wheel so that he can look around himself.

"Full and by, Neil," he tells him.

"Full and by, Skipper, " the bosun repeats.

We always acknowledge orders, that way everyone knows that they've been heard and understood.

We've sunk the land astern now and there's only the blue ocean as far as the eye can see. Our schooner is content. We give her free rein and like a thoroughbred racehorse she takes off as if the devil himself is after her. Standing on the deck we feel her through our feet as she lifts quickly to romp over the long ocean swell rolling in from the north.

Picking up speed, the knot meter reaches ten knots and when she comes out of the roll and her 15,800 square feet of canvas takes the wind square on, she surges ahead. Then the knot meter climbs even higher. This is what we have all waited for; the schooner at sea with the open ocean in front of her and nought to halt her run. She can go for it now, there's nothing to stop her.

The wind is on the best possible angle for the *Bluenose*, just abaft the beam and it's blowing as hard as we need for now. In fact, our lee rail is near the water level and every time she takes a good roll, under it goes. The main deadeyes drag for a moment whipping the sea into a white froth and then she lifts again, shuddering slightly, as if shaking herself before flying on. We all feel exhilaration, a quickening of the pulse. We're standing on a live ocean Valkyrie and she's running wild and hard. There's a roaring white wave under her bow and all along the lee rail the foam rushes past. Inside the bulwarks the merry water rushes back and forth. It comes in over the rail when she dips and goes out through the freeing ports when she lifts. But some always stays to gurgle inside the lee scuppers and from the forward rigging to the break deck there's a slosh of white water. It's roll and go, the old Atlantic schooner dance. The ocean is the dance floor; the wind is the music, and the *Bluenose* moves with the rhythm of the sea. Every time a big swell comes from the windward side, she rolls, and her tall masts lean to leeward, momentarily lessening the area of sail presented to the wind. And then when the swell rolls under her keel, she comes upright again, the wave passing under her keel. When the wind takes her full on, we feel her shake as she takes off again. Over and over, roll and go, roll and go. The sounds of the ocean are with us now, the hiss of the spray as it flies aft and the hissing of the sea foam as it falls away to leeward. There's the creaking of the blocks and the cracks and groans of a sailing ship at sea. Good sounds, real and true.

Our decks are wet now and as the salt spray comes aboard, the wind drives it horizontally over us. It is cold, but we're so excited that we laugh under the bright sun and cloudless sky. The perfect day, the perfect schooner, and the perfect time. A perfect life? Perhaps. I cannot in truth think of any place I'd rather be. All the riches in the world cannot equal the feeling that I have now. It is a feeling that only those who come to the sea before the mast can know. There is a special bond between a man and his sailing ship. Love? Maybe. The special feeling as she lifts unbidden to meet the oncoming sea or the thrill when the knot meters touches supernatural numbers.

And so, as I close my old logbook and gaze out towards the Atlantic over the waters of Mahone Bay, I notice a tear in my eye. This great schooner was my first true love.

*The Dory Man of Cape Sable Island,
pulling around the course.*

The Dory Man of Cape Sable Island

The old fisherman sat by his window overlooking the Atlantic Ocean. His gaze took him far offshore to a place beyond the horizon and for a few moments he pondered his life. Although three score and ten years had passed beneath his keel, it seemed like only yesterday that he was a young man shipping out on a schooner bound for the Grand Banks. But the years had flown like leaves on the wind and his life had been hard. Hard in the way only men who have fished cod from a dory on the Grand Banks can know. This had been his life. Sailing schooners into the great Atlantic and questing for cod on the vast ocean far from land.

Manuel De Silva felt a twinge of sadness come over him. He knew that the time was at hand when this way of life would be only a memory. The young men had gone to the cities to drive taxicabs or work in the shops. The old fisherman's sons had gone out west, where they said the dollars were plentiful and easy.

He knew that there were none to follow in his footsteps, to fish the great schools of cod from longline dories on the Grand Banks. There were none with the passion or strength to pit them themselves against nature in this fashion. He was the last of the schooner dory men.

But now the day he had been waiting for had come. Months before, he had heard along the docks about the great dory race around the island where he lived on Nova Scotia's south shore. Tomorrow, fishermen from nearby bays and coves would row a ten-mile race around Cape Sable Island. It was a long hard race and people said that only the strong young men would row. But the old fisherman thought otherwise.

"I will row this race." he said to himself, "I can do it."

In the years past, Manuel had been renowned in the schooner fleet for being one of the best; a strong rower and a great schooner man.

"I can remember the time my dory was lost on the banks. It was cold and rough, but with my compass I rowed for more than twenty-six hours before they found me." he thought to himself.

He looked down at his gnarled old hands with fingers crooked from holding the oars. They told of more than fifty years rowing dories on the far ocean. He remembered the sea and could almost taste the salty flavor of it. He loved the ocean and he remembered how it was to row upon the great Atlantic. It had been a good life and now for one last time he would row a good row.

He turned to his wife Philomena. She had stood by him all these years.

"I will row that race." he told her. "I can still row well."

"You are a foolish old man" his wife told him, "How do you think you can row around the island against the young men and boys? You are a foolish old man; they will laugh at you."

"They may think I am foolish, but I will row." he replied.

Philomena shook her head. She knew her husband well. If he had set his mind on this, then no one would dissuade him.

"Well then, I will make food for you and water to take." she told him.

The old man slept soundly and woke just before dawn on the day of the race. Getting out of bed he dressed and ate some bread and a piece of cheese. Philomena gave him a large mug of black coffee to drink before leaving.

"Goodbye and safe voyage." his wife told him as she had done a thousand times before.

"Thank you, Philomena."

She knew that whatever Manuel found on the ocean he would row well.

Going outside he took his long banks oars, a small bag of gear, and a bailer for the short walk to the boat launch. His wizened face was creased from the salt of the sea and the sun. He looked old; his seventy years carried on shoulders bent from years of rowing the dories. But there was a determination in his slow steady stride.

The Dory Man of Cape Sable Island

He came to his old dory with oars shipped over his shoulders. All the younger men were at the launch preparing their boats for the great race.

"Manuel, what are you doing?" they asked.

"I will row today." he told them.

They shook their heads. The old man would probably just row around the bay and wait for the other dories to return. They thought Manuel was too old to row very far. He would not even finish the course.

Manuel was well known to them. They called him the old Portege because his ancestors had come from Lisbon in Portugal. They knew and respected him as a man who had spent his life on the great Atlantic.

Soon all was ready, and the men slid their dories into the bay where they bobbed with their sterns close to the shore. Manuel rowed to the edge of the starting line and waited. The man on the dock fired his pistol and the dories flew forward as oars and shoulders bent to their tasks.

The great Atlantic Ocean streamed away to the south in an unending expanse of blue. Soon all the boats pulled well ahead of Manuel's dory and disappeared around the first point of land from the bay. Manuel was alone.

The old fisherman pulled his boat with an easy rhythm and strength borne of a lifetime at sea. He did not have to think, it came naturally. Manuel paused from time to time to take a bearing on the land with his small box compass. He knew the fog could come stalking very quickly.

The sun rose higher in the sky and his dory made good time. The sea was smooth and the wind light. Shipping his oars, he paused for a moment and took a swig of water. Squinting against the sun he thought about the other rowers.

"They are young and fast he said to himself" but they don't know that I can row for twenty-four hours at a time. I have the stamina." he said to himself.

Smiling he took up his oars and began pulling again, his dory gliding almost effortlessly over the sea.

Towards noon, the sky began to cloud over and a few miles to the northeast of Sable Island a lone dory lay bobbing beneath the leaden sky. The wind began to blow stronger from the north and then the sun slid behind the low grey clouds taking any remnants of warmth with it.

Manuel Da Silva sat resting at the oars. He was not yet even halfway around the course and he was beginning to feel tired. His seventy years had begun to weigh heavily upon his shoulders. He was strong still, but only a shadow of the powerful young man who had taken to the sea some three score years before. The years had run their course and he had been on the sea for more years than he cared to remember. Life on a banks schooner was hard and dangerous work; a man's work but he had never flinched. Manuel always seemed to have an inner strength that never failed him.

"How did I come to be here?" he asked himself smiling.

But his heart knew that this was where he was meant to be.

The last headland of the race lay some five miles ahead to the north.

"I must row harder now, before the wind takes me." he said to himself as he took another swig from the water bottle in the bow of the dory, to wash down the bread and cheese Philomena had given him.

"I can still row." he said picking up the oars to begin the long sure stroke that he knew was the best.

Manuel leaned his shoulders to the oars pulling the dory forward against the wind.

"I must just keep moving, there is a long way to go if I am to complete the course today." he murmured.

The other boats were many miles ahead, he thought, but the younger men will tire, and he would catch up.

Manuel looked at his hands. They were bloody. Straining against the wind his oars bent as he pulled, the strong long stroke he knew he needed to keep his dory moving north.

As the afternoon wore on, the waves came up and a nasty chop developed.

"I must keep her bow to it and feather my blades." he reminded himself.

Late in the afternoon, Manuel rounded the last point and began to pull into the bay. The old man knew he had lost the race. But at least inside the bay he knew that had the strength to finish.

THE DORY MAN OF CAPE SABLE ISLAND

He was very tired now and his arms and shoulders hurt. His hands bled but he dipped them in the cold ocean to staunch the bleeding. As he pulled towards the landing, he could not see the dock behind him, but he began to hear a low cheering.

Shipping his oars, he turned to a sight he could not have believed. The other boats had not crossed the line. They had formed a narrow channel four boats to a side and the men signaled for him to row between them.

The old fisherman took his oars in hand and pulled his dory towards the finish line. The other young men stood and waved him on.

"You have won Manuel!" they called to him.

At first, he did not understand, but after a moment he realized. They had not crossed the line. They had let him win. The creases of his face filled with tears as he finally pulled across the line.

The young men took his bow and pulled it up the landing and they helped him out.

Manuel de Silva had won the race.

That evening the fishermen from along the coast and nearby coves came to his small house. The came to listen to him tell of the old ways of dories and schooners. And then they would take a small cup of the strong West Indian rum before leaving.

And so began a legend of the sea. The story of an old fisherman who could not be subdued. A tale of good kind seamen who would not see one of their own left behind. And as the years passed people would speak of that day and of "The Dory Man of Cape Sable Island."

This story is dedicated to all those who have sailed upon the Great Atlantic and especially those who have ever fought their way into the teeth of a November North Atlantic gale.

A whaleboat of yesteryear sails to the west of Bequia.

THE LAST HARPOONER

Morning comes and a light breeze ushers in the first rays of sunlight over Admiralty Bay, rustling the long fronds of the coconut trees surrounding the village of Port Elizabeth. The old man steps from the door of his cottage on the hill and walks slowly down the path towards the white sand beach as he has done every morning since he could remember. Despite his three score and five years, his back is straight and his movements sure. The passage of time has affected his outward appearance, but his heart remains strong.

Sharp eyes peer from beneath a bushy brow and the thick snow-white hair contrasts with his darkly tanned skin. The face is heavily creased by a lifetime in the sun and salt spray. It is a visage of sound character, hinting of a thousand stories waiting to be told. His hands are large and thickly callused, his feet bare, the toes splayed wide from a life without shoes.

He strolls towards the water's edge where the boats are pulled up, carrying his striking iron, a seven-foot shaft of four-inch-thick oiled pine, joined to three feet of half-inch steel rod and tipped with an eight-inch barbed lance which gleams as the light hits it. Despite its heaviness, he manages it with ease. He is a Bequia whaler.

He has launched his thirty-foot wooden whaleboat from the same spot for thirty years. It is the best position on the beach, in front of the Port Elizabeth post office. Although he has never paid for this berth, it is his and no man will question that. He is a harpooner.

Pausing momentarily in front of his boat he places his harpoon in the bow. Then, with a hint of a smile lovingly rubs her stem. The name *Emiline* appears under the rail. It was his wife's name. He will sail her again today as he has done so many times before.

His crew arrives, one with the sail, and others with the oars. But the six whalers are all mature, older men, and all have seen more than half a century pass. Where are the young? They are not here.

The sleek double-ender is launched, and her smooth black bottom kisses the waters of the bay. Pushing from the shore, the crew ships their oars and push from the land, while the harpooner and mate hoist the sails.

The whaleboat leaves the lee of Bequia and moves northwards, into the channel. Tasting the first trade wind gust, her long boomed spritsail and jib fill and she heels before taking off. Soon she is moving with the sea, like a white-winged gull, over crest and down trough. Her crew hike to windward keeping her steady, as her stout hull cleaves the waves. The wind in the channel is fierce and the deep blue Caribbean rolls and breaks in frothy fifteen footers. Heeled well-over, the fast-moving whaleboat sails on.

The island of St. Vincent looms to the north. The whalers are bound for the huge lee to the west of this landmass, where the great sperm whales will be found. They do not waste many words. Each knows what must be done and they go about sailing their craft quietly and efficiently. Her bow dips into a wave, and the warm spray hisses over the caprail into their faces. It is a good feeling.

The whaleboat leaves the last of the rough water behind her and sails into the lee of the island. The wind eases and the sea becomes calm. The high mountains of St. Vincent have created this vast area of smooth water and the hot tropical sun sparkles as it reflects off the surface. The whaleboat is but a tiny speck on the blue expanse as she sails onwards.

To the northwest a lone sperm whale rests on the surface. He has traveled thousands of miles to reach this place. Since the beginning of time, his kind have passed this way on their migrations, and now he will rest on the surface for a while in the great calm, absorbing the warm sun on his scarred back. He blows every few minutes, throwing a telltale marker of white spray above the clear horizon. An old solitary male, his back and flanks are scarred by a hundred battles with other males who have questioned his supremacy and his head and jaws bear deep gashes and gouges where giant squid have wounded him. But he has always won his battles, until now.

The grey whaleboat sails northwards. The harpooner stands in the bow with his left hand on the headstay, while the right shades his eye as he scans the horizon. The sun rises in the sky and as he wipes the residue of dried salt from his face; man and whale are brought closer to their destiny. His keen eye catches a tiny movement a few miles off their port bow.

"Whale blow," he shouts pointing to the northwest.

The helmsman pulls the tiller towards him, and the crew eases the sheets. The whaleboat surges on with the wind on her quarter. As they close the distance, the crew sees the black leviathan basking on the surface, an immense ancient warrior of at least fifty feet. The men experience a quickening of the pulse and there is a tension in the air. Many have died over the years in this pursuit and there is danger ahead.

The harpooner stands in the bow, the lance balanced easily in his hand as he offers directions to the man at the tiller. They close the distance.

The old sperm whale becomes aware of the approaching craft; he can hear the gentle swishing of her wooden hull as it sails though the water. But he is confident, perhaps even disdainful.

At three hundred feet the sails are lowered, and the crew take to the oars. The harpooner urges his crew onwards, and they pace themselves, saving a measure of speed for the last. At one hundred feet, the whale breaches slowly showing his broad flukes before he sounds. But the harpooner does not despair. The whale will go down, but he will surface again along the same path, perhaps five hundred yards along. They row on. The chase is long and hard, but every time the whale sounds it comes up more quickly and less distant. Finally, the time is at hand.

The harpooner raises his harpoon as the rowers instinctively offer up the last of their strength putting a bend in the wooden oars. The great whale blows again this time no more than fifty feet ahead. He slows for a moment as he arches his broad back to dive. The harpooner draws back and the tip of the lance glitters momentarily in the brilliant sunlight.

"Strike!"

The pine shaft leaves his hand as it has done scores of times before, and for a moment he remembers his first. His aim is true, and the lance strikes the whale high in the back burying itself to the hilt of the wooden shaft. The rowers cease gratefully, their work is done. Now the harpooner sits athwart the aft seat and slacks line over the heavy bit through the bow chock.

The whale sounds furiously this time, and his flukes flay the water into a maelstrom of white spray. He cannot understand what has happened, but there is a pain in his chest, and he cannot breathe. He makes for the safety of the blue depths, but after only a few moments he must surface again.

The great whale breaks the smooth surface of the blue Caribbean once more but this time the blow is red with blood. The steel lance has penetrated the lungs and now the leviathan is dying.

The harpooner looks on and nods. There is neither joy nor sorrow in his face. He takes no pleasure in the killing of this animal. It is a way of life, and the whale will support his family and his crew for a long time. He pulls on the harpoon line with his crew and the whale attempts to sound again, but it is a feeble effort.

Soon the whaleboat lies alongside the almost inert whale and the harpooner takes the long killing lance in his hand. He climbs aboard the broad back and his splayed feet find grip on the rubbery surface. He climbs to the highest point and gauges where the huge heart must lie, and then he raises his arm high before driving the killing strike. The whale blows its last and the harpooner is bathed in red. It is over.

Later, the whale is towed to the small station to the southeast of Paget's Farm. The great beast will be processed there, and every part used. There will be no waste. The harpooner stands aside and watches. He has done his work and now the others will do theirs. Soon he will take his crew and sail the *Emiline* back to her place on the sand in Admiralty Bay. The old men of his crew will carry the mast and sails away and he will shoulder his harpoon and walk to his cottage on the hill.

As he ponders the day, a twinge of sadness comes over him. He knows that the time is at hand when this way of life will be only a memory. The young men have gone to the bigger islands to drive taxicabs or work in the shops. The harpooner's sons have gone to America where they say the dollars are plentiful and easy. There are none to follow in his footsteps, to hunt the great whale in the lee of St. Vincent. There are none with the passion or strength to pit them themselves against nature in this fashion. He is the last of the Bequia whalers.

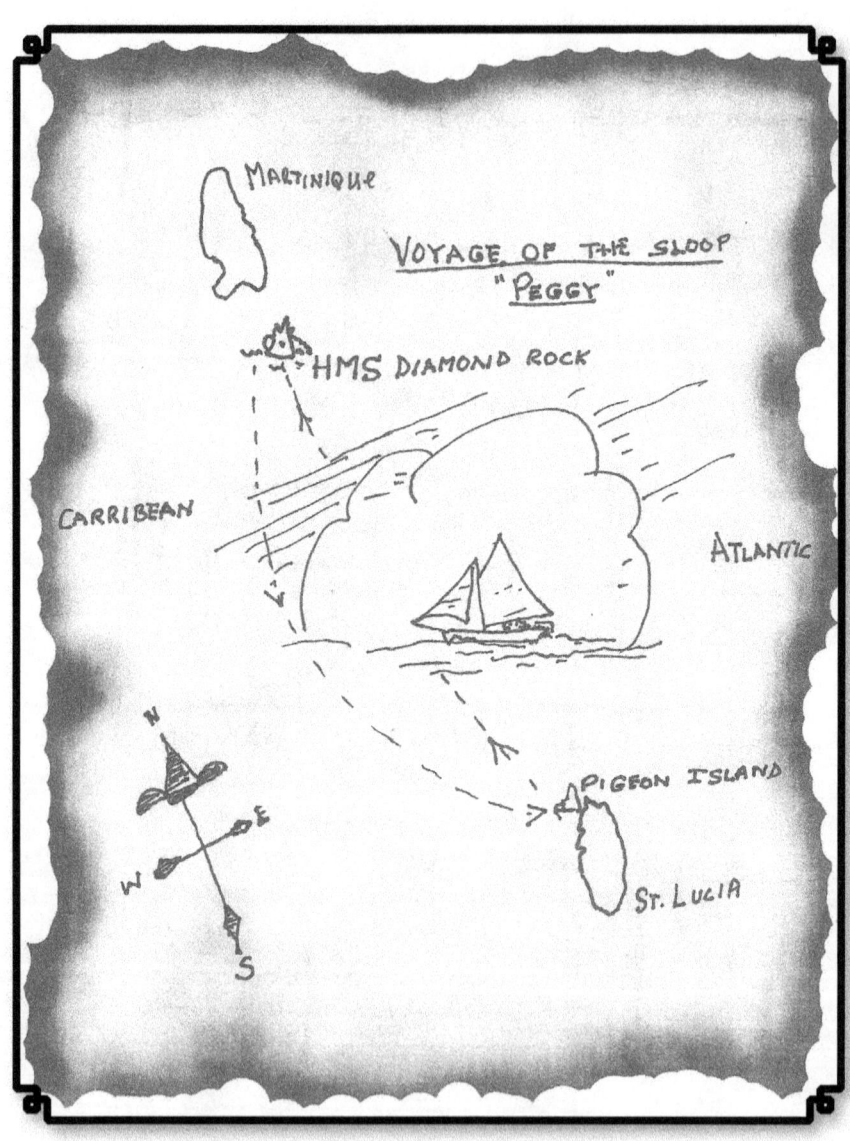

*Our chart showing the Voyage of the Peggy.
Young sailormen on a voyage of adventure.*

HMS DIAMOND ROCK

Growing up in Marigot Bay, St. Lucia during the 1960's was an adventure. There were a few youngsters living in the village overlooking the bay and we quickly befriended them. Lewis Dala was my age and he loved to fish and explore as much as I did. He often sailed with my brothers and I on the Peggy, the twenty-five-foot wooden sloop my father had given us one Christmas.

She was red-hulled with a simple gaff-rigged main and one jib. A small oblong cockpit seated four and a sliding hatch led to the cabin. The *Peggy* was a spartan ship below decks. Just the hull frames and a bench to port and starboard. Nonetheless she sailed very well, and we thought her the best.

The *Peggy* was my first real ship, and we had many adventures in her, but had my parents known where some of our voyages took us, they might have keeled over. We frequently made overnight trips to the bays and coves along the coast and usually held firm to the destinations our father had plotted out for us.

One summer's day when I was fourteen, we planned an overnight voyage to Pigeon Island at the north end of St. Lucia. With my brother Peter as mate and Lewis as deckhand we stocked the *Peggy* with a container of fried chicken, bread, and water, and set off on yet another exploit.

It was a fine day; a blue trade wind sky hung overhead filled with puffy white clouds. The easterly breeze tossed spray over the bow as we laid a course northward from Marigot Bay. Our little red-hulled sloop danced merrily over the waves dipping her lee rail occasionally. Before we knew it, we were miles offshore and well past the point that dad had instructed was the safe limit. As I looked to the north, the island of Martinique and Diamond Rock suddenly seemed very close.

"Pete," I said excitedly, "let's go to Diamond Rock."

My brother looked at me with a little uncertainty. The rock lay some nineteen miles from St. Lucia and was most definitely out of our bounds.

"Do you think it'll be okay?" he asked, although the tone of his voice told me he already knew the answer.

"Yes man, come on, we'll be there real quick today." I persuaded, surprised when he agreed.

I was the one usually tagged for hatching illegal schemes in the family and being the oldest usually got in trouble for "knowing better." Lewis, on the other hand, had no qualms about voicing his uncertainty. His superstitions about the open sea ran deep.

"De deeper de wata, de more dangerous it is." he said.

"That not true." I said, "How deep has nothing to do with it."

"That's what you think. In the deep have sea devils. Plenty people disappear already. Look, you remember Una, de fisherman? He went fishing in de deep last year and he never come back."

It was no use. Pete and I out-voted him, and in any case, he was out-ranked. We closed the distance rapidly and before long Diamond Rock was closer to us than the big French island. The formidable citadel rose precipitously from the sea, growing in size as our little ship approached. Stone cliffs dotted with black-mouthed caves appeared and jagged precipices overhung the sea. Suddenly I felt a stinging sense of uncertainty. Pete and I had seen Diamond Rock from the deck of our father's schooner many times, but now it was different. Alone, our confidence waned. Massive rocks ascended from the dark blue depths to only a few feet below the surface, reaching toward our keel.

"That's a big rock, man." Pete breathed.

"Yeah. Let's go and explore it." I suggested with false bravado, "You know, this is where all those soldiers died. Right up there."

Lewis didn't let that go by.

"You crazy man? You mean it have dead people deah?"

I convinced him they were indeed dead, and had been for quite some time, and although I'd failed to quell my own secret fears, I managed to quell his.

My father had once told us the tragic tale of Diamond Rock, and I remembered his words.

HMS Diamond Rock

"Years ago, when the British and the French were fighting over the islands, a terrible thing happened here. The main port for French warships making landfall in Martinique is just around the corner in Fort de France. The British Admirals thought that if they could keep the French ships from sailing close along the shore, as they approached from the east, they would have to stand offshore, ending up far to the leeward of Fort de France. The great frigates were square rigged and didn't sail into the wind very well. They could lose days tacking back up into Fort de France.

The British decided to put cannons on Diamond Rock to keep the French warships offshore. It was one of history's great feats of seamanship and engineering. The British sailed one of their frigates up to the rock, moored her there, and hoisted the heavy cannons to the top. They built a rain catchment with cistern, fortifications, and quarters for the men to live. When it was all done the British put a garrison of their soldiers ashore and called the fort *HMS Diamond Rock*.

At first, the plan worked well; whenever a French ship tried to sail in under the protection of the coast towards the harbor of Fort de France, it was driven offshore by the British guns. But the British success was short lived. The French had been busy too, and they brought bigger guns to bear from the hills of Martinique, preventing the British frigates from supplying their soldiers on Diamond Rock.

Time passed and drought prevailed. Food was scarce on the rock and the fair-skinned Brits suffered terribly in the heat. They slowly succumbed to thirst and starvation, yet the Union Jack continued to wave from the heights of the rock. The British still call it *HMS Diamond Rock*, and to this day, whenever Her Majesty's warships pass by, they dip their flag in a salute to the men who perished there.

Even as I thought about my father's story, Pete came up with a plan to moor the *Peggy*, suggesting we drop anchor and take a line ashore at the base of the rock.

"We all go dead, you know dat?" Lewis said, again voicing his grave doubts about the wisdom of this escapade. "We all go dead. Why you have to come to dis place? Everybody know dat it have very bad spirits."

"Don't worry, Lewis." Pete piped in with renewed brevity, "it'll be good fun."

We dropped the jib and sailed our little sloop up to a point in the calmest lee of *HMS Diamond Rock*. Pete dropped the main and Lewis pitched the little Danforth anchor overboard. As we furled the sails, the eerie silence was almost haunting. The immensity of the rock, if not our tryst, now fully dawned upon me.

The perks of rank have their benefits and it fell to Lewis, as the lowest ranking crewmember, to swim ashore with the stern line.

"Boy, you crazy. Ah ain goin in dis wata. Look down dey, it blue, blue, blue."

"Go on, Lewis. Don't be a baby." we cajoled him.

After a few moments with both Pete and myself staring at him, Lewis gave a big snort and dove in. Swimming ashore, he climbed onto a small stone ledge at the water's edge. It looked as though it had been carved in the rock on purpose, for use as a landing point perhaps. Lewis tied the line around an outcrop of stone, and we hauled our stern in close. Pete and I went ashore as well, but no amount of talking would keep Lewis on the rock. He scrambled back aboard the *Peggy* the first chance he got and positioned himself firmly in the hatchway where he nibbled hungrily on a chicken drumstick, watching us from a safe distance. If he was about to die at the hands of some sort of devil on the rock, he wasn't going without some of Ma Boudreau's chicken first.

The sun was hot as Pete and I began ascending the perilous stone-strewn path that climbed drunkenly upwards. The rock was barren with only a few prickly cactus plants and dry sandy earth. It was obvious that little rain fell here. A few lizards scurried out of our way and a multitude of sea birds appeared following us upwards. They screeched and dove over our heads as if telling us to leave that we had no right to put our feet on this their place of bravery and suffering long past.

Pete shouted out first. "Hey Lou, come and see this."

He was bending over a bush on the side of the path. Stooping down beside him we brushed away the dry sand from a long piece of rusted metal.

"It's a gun, man." My brother shouted picking up the barrel of an old musket rifle.

As he shook away the years of sand I marveled that his treasure was being held in the hands of a living being for the first time in more than a century. I tried to imagine who had been the last and how he had died. Holding it out as if to fire it Pete sighted along the barrel. The wood had long since gone but at that moment it was real enough to us.

We climbed further before coming to the area where the soldiers had lived and died. An old stone water cistern and living quarters had been built into the side of the rock. We found many treasures that day. Brass sword hilts with heavily rusted steel blades, and pistol barrels with the flintlock firing mechanisms. There were white leather straps from uniforms preserved by the dry sand and hot sun. We collected dozens of musket balls and a few cannon balls. There were scores of these, but because of their weight we could not carry many. I found brass buttons from officer's tunics and a long-stemmed white clay pipe.

As I stood there in the ramparts of *HMS Diamond Rock* with a rusty pistol in one hand and the remnants of a sword, I felt a strange sensation come over me. There were indeed ghosts here. The story of the place echoed in my ears and as I closed my eyes for a moment I could hear my father's voice.

"They all died you know. There was no way to help them or get water to them."

I saw the soldiers then, in their red tunics with white straps standing in the sun. They stood bravely facing the north towards Martinique with their muskets leveled.

Peter shook me out of my daydream.

"Look down there, Lou."

I looked downwards to where Pete was pointing. From where we stood our sloop looked like a tiny red dot on the water next to the base of the cliff. The sun was halfway down the sky and Lewis was waving from the safety of the hatch. It was time for us to go and we scampered down the rocky pathway to the landing. Lewis met us there and was worried about the things we had brought down from the heights.

"I tellin you Lou, dem tings is dead people tings an you should trow dem in de sea."

"No man, these are neat, look here." I brandished a sword hilt, and Lewis cowered as if he had seen a ghost.

Casting off from the shore, we set the main before getting the anchor up. It wasn't long before we were on our way again, the *Peggy* heeling once again to the easterly breeze, bound for the peaks of Pigeon Island which we could see some twenty miles distant.

As we sailed, it was time for reflection. There had been much during the day that was new to us, and another new experience was soon to come. Although we had done a lot of sailing we always planned to be anchored at night. Now, as the last rays of light from the setting sun died to the west, we felt very alone on the greatness of the sea. It would be very dark soon and we were far from land. The *Peggy* had no compass or lights and Lewis had eaten all the chicken while we were ashore. Pete and I sat in the cockpit and ate bread washed down with water from the plastic container; it tasted surprisingly good. Pete steered and as the completeness of tropical darkness fell upon us, the stars came out in their millions dotting the sky in an impossible array of splendor. We soon saw the glow of Castries town and steered our course accordingly.

Pete and I talked through the night with the stars as our guide. We talked about the fish, the birds, and the sea. We wondered about the massif, which had disappeared in the darkness astern of us so many hours past, the men, the living, and the dying. As we talked, we held the old bits of sword and pistol in our hands. The great trade winds blew gently, and two young boys spoke of great things.

The *Peggy* anchored in Pigeon Island as the sun rose. The wind had turned light during the night and our little sloop had glided slowly across the Martinique channel. We slept the day, except for Lewis who had slept the night. He had been terrified of sea spirits and would not come on deck. The only sign of his presence had been the occasional noise coming from the cabin as his body dealt with the indigestion of eating more than a dozen pieces of chicken.

We told the story that we had found the artifacts on the other side of Pigeon Island. Our father and mother accepted this, but not without some doubt.

The famous rock is still saluted by British war ships passing by.

I looked at life in a different light after my flying fish chase.

THE FLYING FISH

The Virgin Islands lie just to the east of Puerto Rico stretching some forty miles from the west end of St Thomas to the wreck strewn reefs to the east of Anegada. This beautiful archipelago offers easy sailing and abundant safe anchorages. In the sixties there were a few small restaurants in palm-fringed bays, and we found the area to be a cruisers paradise. To the benefit of our charter clients the sheltered water enjoyed fair winds and calm passages making for a minimum of the mal de mer.

In August 1966, I was a deckhand on the 138-foot schooner *Ramona* while she was chartering in the U.S. and British Virgin Islands. It was the summer holidays, and I was crewing for my father, Captain Walter.

As the ship lay anchored in Charlotte Amalie harbor, St. Thomas, we prepared for our next trip. The schooner was a hive of activity, with the ten crew polishing brass, scrubbing the teak decks, and dressing up the accommodations for the guests. Uniforms were sent to the laundry and the cook made countless trips to market provisioning the ship. The day before the charter, we went alongside the dock for an hour to fuel up and top off our water tanks.

At nine the following morning, I took the newly scrubbed launch to the marina dock, along with two of the other deckhands. Dressed in our white tee shirts, with the name *Ramona* emblazoned across the front, we met our party of eight. After shaking hands, we escorted our guests and their luggage aboard and ferried them out to the waiting schooner. I made a large circle to starboard before bringing the launch gently alongside the boarding ladder, so that our guests could have a look at her long sweeping lines. The morning sun reflected off the water to play on her white hull and she looked impressive and beautiful. All her flags were flying. From the club burgee on the main topmast, to the red British duster on the stern, the *Ramona* looked smart and ready for sea. The steward soon had our party settled in their cabins and after heaving the anchor we headed out of the harbor.

By noon, we were proceeding along the southeast coast of St. John's, with the Anegada passage to our south. We were bound for the Treasure Point anchorage at Norman Island where we planned to lay over for the night. There was not a breath of wind, and the *Ramona* was rolling quite a bit. There wasn't any point in putting sail up, as the gear would just slat around without the wind, so we proceeded under power.

Our charter party was a friendly New York family by the name of Rabinowitz. There was the father, mother, two sons, their wives and two grandchildren. As we powered along, two of the men amused themselves by trolling a fishing line over the stern, while the ladies applied suntan lotion and lay on the deck. The kids played cards in the pilothouse.

The warm Caribbean sun beat down on the schooner as we made our way slowly over the mirror-like sea. An occasional predatory fish broke the surface chasing some unseen prey, and large schools of silvery flying fish flew away from our bows. Sometimes they traveled a hundred yards or more before plopping back into the blue sea. Quite often though, these ten-inch-long fish would mistakenly fly aboard the schooner, and although this happened more during the night, we would occasionally watch them flop to the deck during the day as well. In both cases they were quickly collected and brought to the cook who would then fry them up.

Mrs. Rabinowitz was in her fifties and a rather buxom lady with certain assets, which were wont to overflow her blue flowered bathing suit, despite her hopeless attempts to corral them. I tried desperately to avert my eyes, but they seemed drawn like magnets every time I passed by. They were a compelling sight for a teenage boy.

Later that afternoon she positioned herself in one of the deck chairs on the port side near the rail. She seemed to teeter quite a bit each time the *Ramona* took a roll.

"Lou," my father called me aside. "Go and tie a line around that chair before she goes over, will you?"

Going over with a couple of sail ties in hand I lashed the bottom and top of the chair to one of the stout caprail stanchions.

THE FLYING FISH

"Why, thank you young man." she smiled batting her eyelashes.

Mrs. Rabinowitz was very appreciative but as I walked away, she suddenly let out the most horrible howl. Looking back, I saw her fall from the chair to the deck where she lay flat on her back on the deck waving her arms frantically.

"Help," she cried, "It's getting me!"

Stooping over her I tried to determine what was wrong, but I couldn't see anything.

"Oh, my God!" she cried again, "help!"

Desperately trying not to look at her huge breasts my gaze was inexorably drawn there, and I saw what the problem was. There, sticking out of her ample cleavage was the tail of a small flying fish, wiggling like crazy.

The captain who was still aft at the wheel was growing impatient.

"What the hell's is going on there, Lou?" he called out to me.

I pointed to her breasts and my father frowned. He was puzzled.

The stricken lady was still waving her arms helplessly in the air and crying out. Realizing that I had to act I grabbed the little fish by the tail, but it was stuck and didn't want to come out. Every time I pulled its tail, it just seemed to wriggle further down into her costume, causing Mrs. Rabinowitz more agitation and distress.

There comes a time in every boy's life when he just has to take the plunge and so I did. Taking a deep breath, I dove in there with my right hand until I could get a proper grip on the slippery little fellow. I had to chase it down pretty far and ended up elbow deep in her bathing costume. Just at that moment, Mr. Rabinowitz came down the deck and taking in the scene, leveled me a stern look.

"Look here, young man...." he started growling at me, but before he could finish, I pulled my hand out and stood up proudly displaying the little culprit for all to see. I seem to remember saying something foolish like "Don't worry, it's just a flying fish!"

After this embarrassing incident (for a young lad like me anyway), I kept clear of Mrs. Rabinowitz for the remainder of the cruise, but whenever I accidentally caught her eye, she would smile sweetly and give me a wink.

The Marlin jumps astern of me.

Alone on the Great Atlantic

I had just turned seventeen and I was in the fishing business. Although I was born in Baddeck, Nova Scotia, I had grown up in the West Indies where my father Captain Walter Boudreau had moved his "Nova Scotia Windjammer cruises" and two schooners, Ramona and Caribee.

With the captain's help, I bought a 25-foot skiff. It was a lapstrake Caribe design, built in Trinidad for the local fishing industry. It was narrow with a sweeping sheer and high bow. A good sea boat, she was also equipped with four across thwart seats with positive foam flotation. I knew that even with my smaller 25 hp Johnson motor she would never sink if swamped. My gear consisted of a pair of large oars and a little box compass. I would fish the rich water just north of the island for the plentiful mahi-mahi, wahoo, and tuna that were found there. I sold my catch at $0.35 a pound EC (eastern Caribbean dollar).

One morning I left Marigot Bay with two five-gallon tanks of fuel bound for the north end of the island. At dawn, I was off Pigeon Island, and I sped quickly past the Point Du Cap tip at the north end of the island and into the blue of the great Atlantic. Soon I was clear of the land and the choppy coastal water. I continued about ten miles until I thought I was far enough out. My skiff rode the small waves easily and if I kept her speed down, she was quite comfortable. At about 8 knots or so, she was happy, and it was the right speed to troll. Big silvery footlong flying fish were plentiful, and I could see them almost continuously as they flew from wave to wave.

"Below them are the big ones" I said to myself.

Far from the land the ocean was blue and crisp. The waves, although large, rolled under the keel of my skiff and the windblown spume of the crests blew off into my face. Soon, my body was caked with a fine white salty powder.

UNDER THE TRADE WIND SKY

The islands of Martinique and St Lucia seemed far away to the west. Green smudges on the horizon, I was alone on the great blue Atlantic and I felt at home. Short waves and the occasional white crest surrounded my skiff. I knew that should my outboard ever go wrong, that I would be able to hoist the short mast and jib that I had rigged and sail downwind to the island. It would always be so. The trade winds blew endlessly from the northeast, and I was safe. I rigged my baits. Two braided hand lines of two-hundred-pound test and flying fish bait that I had put in the schooners ice box days before.

I was looking for one of two things; either a "Bois" (raft of thick seaweed) or a flock of feeding sea birds and I found both. The large raft of weed and a dead tree branch was sure to hold predator fish. Flying fish and smaller baitfish found safety under the deep-sea float and as a result, larger fish were sure to be nearby. I would troll around the raft until I got a strike.

A flock of birds drifted about a quarter mile to the north, and I headed that way. The birds were diving on a school of baitfish that was being attacked from below. I could see the agitated surface of the water as the eight-inch flying fish scattered to escape the predators below. Then there were huge splashes as the bigger fish broke surface. Before long I had my first strike.

I caught two mahi-mahi of about 25 pounds each, and one of 90 pounds, six small 12-pound tuna, or bonito as we called them, soon followed. I fished by hand then; there were no rods and reels.

To me this was the greatest adventure. I felt truly free on the ocean and at peace with the sea. Instinctively, I always fought my fish sitting down. I stood up in the skiff only if I had to. Even smaller fish were gaffed and lifted over the side.

Towards noon, the snap twine holding one of my lines popped telling me I had a fish on. As I touched the heavy braided line, I knew it was a big one. I quickly coiled the other line forward, stopped the outboard, and began to fight my fish.

"Should have brought gloves like Dad told me? I am a damn fool."

I knew it was not a tuna, as they tended to sound deep and sulk in the depths when hooked. This one swam broadly from one side to another at no more than twenty-foot depth.

"A big fish. I will see you soon enough." I said to myself smiling.

I had stopped the boat and I drifted slowly into the channel between the Martinique and St Lucia islands. I braced my feet on the gunwale above the sea as I held the line in my hands. The fish was heavy, as heavy as I had ever felt.

"What have I caught here?"

The fish had been swimming just below the surface now for two hours. And the hot afternoon sun shimmered off the water. Every time I tried to take a few feet on him he would take it back. Towards three in the afternoon, he broke surface. And I knew then what was on my line.

The large billfish came clear out of the Atlantic in two broad thirty-foot jumps before crashing back into the blue. He was majestic, blue on top with silver sides, and a tall dorsal fin above his shoulders. I felt fear then. This fish was beyond anything I had ever hooked before.

"I wish my father was here with me." I said to myself, "he would know what to do."

But I was alone with the blue ocean and this great fish.

Towards late afternoon, I had managed to bring him in a bit but then he made a mad rush and took line back. The heavy chord cut my hands deeply and they began to bleed. I dipped them in the water and took a piece of rag from the bottom of the seat and wrapping it around my right hand, began to fight the fish again.

"How much longer can he fight like this?" I thought. "He has to be tired by now."

Later in the afternoon he tired, and I began to bring him in. My arms were weak, and my hands hurt.

"So, now I need to gaff you" I thought to myself.

I could see the great fish then; it was a big marlin. He must have been 10 feet long and 300 pounds, I guessed. I imagined the faces back home when they saw this great fish. But fate had written another ending to this adventure. At the last moment, when his jaw hit the side of the skiff, he broke free, and I watched him swim slowly into the depths. I retrieved the leader and hook and after laying them in the bow I began motoring back to Point du Cap, St Lucia. I reached Marigot Bay just before dark and tied up alongside the schooner.

My father met me at the rail and shouted for one of the deckhands to help clean the other smaller fish.

"What happened, Lou?" my father asked as he saw my bloody hands and he brought me below to the galley where he washed them with fresh water.

"What happened to your hands, Lou?" he asked again.

"I caught a big fish and I got it to the boat before it got off." I replied.

I knew by the way he looked me in the eye that he believed me.

It was but a short space in time when a young lad faced a challenge on the great Atlantic. I did not need to kill that fish and today as I approach my 70th year, I am happy that the fish got off to live another day.

As I write this, I can close my eyes and see the great fish leave the sea in long arcs under the Caribbean sun. Perhaps someday my son will relive this memory under a trade wind sky on a calm blue sea.

Janeen Leaving St. Lucia for the Grenadines and the Tobago Cays.

THE REEF

In the winter of 1975, we sailed the 138-foot Herreshoff schooner *Janeen* (now the *Mariette*), to the Grenadines. We had just picked up a charter party in St. Lucia, a repeat client who typically stayed with us three or four weeks.

The cruise started off well, and with a stiff breeze off the quarter the schooner made a very fast run between the Pitons of St. Lucia and the north end of St. Vincent averaging 14.5 knots. The following day found us anchored in the Tobago Cays.

Even though this was one of the favorite anchorages of the day, it was still unusual to find more than one or two yachts there at any one time and we were often alone. Horseshoe and Worlds End reefs surrounded the four tiny cays, providing protection from the Atlantic swell. Our party requested we stay there for a few days to snorkel the coral gardens and not being on any schedule, we obliged.

On our second evening in the Cays, while the guests sipped cocktails on the stern, I sat forward with the captain and my brother Pete, enjoying a small rum before sundown. Spotting a sail to the northeast of Horseshoe Reef, I picked up the binoculars to have a closer look. It was a small sloop on a south westerly course, and certainly in an odd position for that time of day. Her skipper would have a hard time seeing the reef ahead of them because the sun was low in the sky and right in their eyes.

We began to worry that if the sloop didn't change course quickly, it would hit the reef. It wasn't a particularly rough day, but the water on the eastern side of that coral had a few thousand miles of open ocean behind it and there was a long, low swell rolling gently in.

Sure enough, as we watched through the glasses, the little sloop hit and bounced up over the reef, coming to rest on her side in a shallow patch of coral.

Although it would soon be dark, my father the captain decided to send Pete and me off in the fourteen-foot Whaler to help. So, starting the outboard we left, accompanied by another of the deckhands. It was a good three-quarters of a mile to the stranded vessel.

We were about halfway there when we noticed some activity on the stranded sloop. In the fading light I saw an orange life raft pop up alongside. It drifted downwind towards us and soon we were alongside. Pulling aside the flap on the brightly colored canopy we found a man cowering on the rubber floor, He was shaking like a leaf.

"Are you alright?" I asked him concerned.

He managed to utter a feeble "yes." and we lifted him out by the arms setting him down in the bottom of the Whaler. He was wet and cold.

Dragging the two-person inflatable raft over the bow, we returned to the *Janeen*. It was dark by then, but we got our survivor aboard and hoisted the rubber raft to the schooner's foredeck. Taking him below we gave him dry clothes and coffee, but he seemed pretty dazed and unable to speak. We figured he was probably an amateur sailor, taking this misadventure very hard. I was still trying to find out his name when the captain called me back on deck.

"What do you make of that?" he asked pointing out towards the reef. A tiny light waved slowly back and forth.

"It looks as though somebody's still aboard." I replied surprised.

"You'd better get back out there and find out what's going on." he told me.

I knew that it wasn't going to be easy getting back out to the sloop in the dark, but the wind had died down a bit with nightfall, as it usually did in those latitudes, and the swell would be down as well. Pete and I took off again, accompanied by the deckhand and a pair of powerful flashlights.

Cautiously working our way into the shallows to leeward of the wreck, we were amazed to hear a woman's voice.

"Help, help me please!"

She was waving a flashlight, which was lucky indeed because it was very dark, and we would have had the devil's own time trying to find her otherwise.

THE REEF

"We're coming, hold on." Pete reassured her.

I steered carefully through the reef, guided by the two torch lights and we neared the wrecked sloop. From the bow our deckhand fended off the coral heads with an oar, while Pete did the same from the stern. We managed to get the Whaler right up to the stranded yacht without damage, and sure enough, there was a woman in a yellow life jacket sitting on the lee side and very glad to see us.

"Thank you," she gasped. "Thank you, thank you."

We took her aboard and carefully made our way back out through the reef. Soon we were motoring back towards the *Janeen* for the second time. We gave the poor shivering woman a towel and through chattering teeth she told us her story.

Susan and her husband Bob had left Miami a month earlier and were cruising their new forty-footer for the first time in the islands. Apparently, their misfortune was a result of inexperience and a bit of bad judgment. As she told us about her husband she burst into tears. Susan had last seen him in the cockpit just before the sloop hit the reef. She had fallen down the companionway and hit her head, knocking herself out. When she finally came around, her husband was gone.

"Bob must have drowned when the boat hit." she wailed.

"But your husband is alive," I told her. "He's on our schooner. We picked him up in the life raft."

"The life raft?" she said looking puzzled.

"Yes, you know, the life raft from your boat," I explained.

The grief she had been feeling for the loss of her husband turned to joy and her tears disappeared.

She was sitting there quietly as we came alongside the *Janeen*, but even as she climbed the boarding ladder, our shipwreck survivor was putting two and two together. She exploded only a moment after reaching the deck.

"You rotten bastard," she shouted angrily. "Where are you?"

Luckily for Bob, he was still in shock down below in the crew's mess hall.

"You left me out there." She was really screaming now and scanning the dimly lit faces on deck to see if she could recognize her hubby.

In the moments of panic after the sloop hit, Bob had jumped off in the survival raft, abandoning his wife. She was understandably mad as hell. Susan spat out exactly what she was going to do when she got hold of him and it wasn't going to be very pretty. In all my born days, I have never seen anyone so enraged.

We felt it prudent to keep them apart that night and arranged bunks for them in different areas of the ship. Our charter party took it all in their stride and eventually we all went to bed.

The next day the police boat came up from Union and the sloop was pulled off with little damage. As we ferried Bob and a still furious Susan over to the police boat in the Whaler, I recalled a line of half humorous doggerel. "Women and children first, except when it comes to drowning, then it's every man for himself."

Bob must have written it.

We fought Pirates of the Caribbean and here we sit on the foredeck after the incident. The other guns we had are in the pilot house.

Pirates of the Caribbean

In the early 1980s, we sailed the High Barbaree from the Virgin Islands to Florida for a refit. There were rumors of drug pirates in the Bahamas, and actual statistics sufficient to cause some anxiety. Many yachts chose to carry firearms to defend themselves and we were no exception.

Prior to leaving, we spoke with the Coast Guard in St. Thomas.

"Be prepared and alert at all times." they advised. "Most people who get into trouble have no idea whatsoever that they might be getting into a dangerous situation."

Evidently, the pirates found the unarmed and friendly yachtsmen quite a bonus. A mode of transportation free for the taking, which could be commandeered at any point along their route and disposed of easily when they were through with it.

The authorities gave us some background as to how the drug pirates operated. A hijacking could take many different forms and depended largely on the circumstances, but of the cases so far recorded, there were some chilling examples.

The most common "modus operandi" was to attack a yacht in the open sea, where there would be no witnesses. They would come alongside in a fast boat, kill the people aboard and take over the yacht. The Bahamas lent itself well to this method because vast expanses of calm, sheltered water abounded, where yachts on passage would be found alone.

Another reported method was for the pirates to set a life raft in the path of an oncoming yacht with some armed pirates posing as shipwreck survivors hiding inside. A distress flare might be used to attract the yacht. When the flare is spotted, the captain calls all hands on deck. The crew lines the rail as they come alongside the raft but then the two rough looking "survivors" suddenly jump up with guns in hand. They have no problem dispatching the yacht crew; they have conveniently lined themselves up along the rail like targets at a shooting gallery. The hijacked craft could then be loaded and sailed into the United States.

Initially, cruising yachts were considered less suspicious by the authorities, and it was easy to sail into a Florida port with no one bothering you. Unfortunately, the crews of the yachts were considered expendable, and many remain unaccounted for.

It is interesting to note here that the northern section of the Bahamas is included in the mysterious "Bermuda Triangle." Case files of yachts and ships lost in this area have often been closed with nothing more than "missing, presumed lost at sea" printed on the folder. Personally, I believe that the main reason for the higher numbers of maritime "disappearances" in this area can be chalked up to the very high density of marine traffic there. But drug smugglers would find it very convenient having any yachts they sink in the Gulf Stream being reported as "Lost in the Bermuda Triangle."

The Coast Guard officers in St. Thomas added finally that if firearms were going to be a part of our inventory, we should know how to use them and have them accessible at all times. It would be no good shouting, "Honey, where did we stow the bullets?" as the attackers came barreling down the hatch!

Finally, they pointed out that when it came right down to it, the drug pirates don't want to die. They want to be around to enjoy their ill-gotten gains. So, if a situation arose where their prospective "victims" were well-armed and prepared to fight, they might be less inclined to press home an attack.

My father, Captain Walter, resolved that we would arm ourselves sufficiently well so that we could protect ourselves in case of an attack. This may sound a little theatrical, but when there were yachts and their crew disappearing under suspicious circumstances, the captain wanted to make sure that our names weren't added to the missing persons list. So, we took stock of our armory. One 9 mm Mauser infantry rife; one 12-gauge semi-automatic shotgun; one .308 Remington hunting rifle and one .45 caliber pistol. Plus, a whole lot of ammunition.

The end of May saw us en route to Florida with a total of eight crew. We lost no time learning how to use our guns and each crewmember fired numerous rounds at empty containers thrown from the bow. The firearms were kept secured in the pilothouse with ready ammunition.

The *High Barbaree* made a fast passage from the Virgins to Great Inagua and apart from one night, just north of Tortuga, when we encountered some very high seas, we enjoyed fine weather. A day later, we passed west of Acklins and Crooked Island. There was no wind and we powered north at about seven and a half knots with no sail set.

The following morning, a dark green trawler appeared about five miles astern of us. After half an hour, she came around to match our course. About three miles away she lined up astern and her bow wave rose as she cracked on speed to catch up. My father began to worry and calling all hands on deck, we took turns looking through the binoculars.

Long Island lay to the southwest and although we could see the shore, there was no chance of making any landfall as there were no safe harbors on the windward side of the island, and so we motored on.

The trawler approached to within three hundred yards, and we began to pick out the details on her deck. She was seventy-five or eighty feet long and resembled the wooden types built in the southern United States for the gulf shrimp fishery. The pilothouse was situated forward, aft of which stood the steel fishing masts and rigging. Vessels of this type and size were usually fitted with big Caterpillar or General Motors diesels and could make a good ten to twelve knots.

We saw the periodic flash of binocular lenses through the pilothouse windows, but so far we had seen no one. Her fishing booms were out but they weren't pulling any nets. However, the vessel appeared to have a full load as she was sitting low in the water.

At two hundred yards our pursuer slowed down, and for the next hour they held their distance. We altered course to see if she would follow and she matched our every move. The captain ordered our weapons out and we carefully loaded them, putting extra ammunition aside. It was just like the drills we had conducted, and everyone knew what to do.

I felt anxious, unable to believe this could really be happening. Gone was the usual light banter between the crew. We were all silent now, and the sound of the main engine exhaust seemed very loud in our ears.

Towards mid-afternoon, the trawler began closing the distance between us and we increased speed to about nine knots. It had developed into one of those hot Bahamian days with a clear sky, flat sea, and not a breath of wind. We would get no help from our sails, so we left them furled. I was dubious as to how long our trusty, but aging engine was going to hold up at full throttle. We were still a long way away from Rum Cay, where we planned to spend the night.

When she was two hundred and fifty feet off, we saw three or four people in the pilothouse of the trawler looking at us through binoculars. A bearded man stepped outside and briefly looked at us before ducking back in.

There was no doubt by this time that the trawler was attempting to do something, but I still found it hard to believe they were actually going to try and hijack us. Then we all saw something that really put the fear of God into us. The bearded man stepped out again, but this time he had a gun cradled in his arms. He stood at the rail looking at us, talking back into the pilothouse. It was almost as if he wanted us to see that he was armed.

We had to do something then. Whatever it was they were going to do, they were getting ready to do it and we couldn't run fast enough to get away. The captain put the vessel on autopilot and the armed crew of the *High Barbaree* moved to the after deck with our guns in hand.

Although we held our weapons aloft so the crew of the trawler could see them, we were ready to jump for cover if they made any threatening moves. They held their position two hundred feet astern of us, but we decided that if they got any closer, we would fire.

We had a good VHF radio but weren't able to get through to anyone. Late in the afternoon, there was some activity on the trawler, and she sped up, coming closer.

We opened fire together. I aimed from behind the steel cockpit coaming as the shotgun and .308 barked from the other side of the deck. We aimed for the trawler's waterline and while the two rifles were hitting the bow area, the shotgun raised splashes of water wildly ahead of her. We quickly fired off more than twenty rounds each and the rifle barrels got hot. The crew of the trawler did not return fire, but they slowed down, dropping back to a respectable distance. We stopped firing.

Not being trained soldiers, it was a strange feeling to be firing these powerful and dangerous weapons at something other than empty oilcans, but at the same time we knew that our lives were in peril.

There was a respite until dusk when we began to close the island of Rum Cay. The trawler made another attempt then and came to within about one hundred feet. We opened fire again and this time we were so close that I could see the splinters of wood fly as each shot hit. The 00 shotgun buck was hitting her bow this time too, leaving large areas of bare wood, but the bullets caused little damage to the heavily constructed vessel.

This time the bearded man on the trawler fired back. Three times he jumped out from the safety of his pilothouse, firing wild bursts from his automatic weapon.

"Fire at the pilothouse!" Captain Walter shouted.

None of the bullets from the trawler had hit us yet, but it would take only one. I aimed carefully and as I pulled the trigger one of the glass windows in the trawler's pilothouse exploded in a shower of broken glass. They were no more than seventy-five feet from our stern now.

"Keep firing," the captain yelled, "Don't stop.

I felt we must give it our all now and try to keep the men from being able to fire at us at such close range. The twelve-gauge shotgun found its mark now too and another of the pilothouse windows burst inwards. The men on the trawler hid inside, but they continued to fire at us, and we ducked as one short burst hit our stern and the mizzenmast. The bullets hitting the steel made a quick ping, ping, ping sound surprisingly like the sound one hears in the movies, but this was no movie, it was real. Some finger sized chunks of varnished spruce fell to the deck around us where they had hit the mizzenmast. We continued to fire at the trawler until our ammunition was nearly finished. When buying the ammunition in St. Thomas, I never realized quite how quickly it would be used. We fired a few final rounds as the trawler backed off and they stopped firing at us. They would never know how close we had come to running out of bullets.

As dusk fell, we closed the last mile to Rum Cay and the trawler finally broke away, altering course to the north. We were terribly shaken by this ordeal, although it didn't affect us until after it was over, and we had put our weapons down. We could see the lights of two other yachts anchored in Rum Cay and made radio contact with one of them as we approached the anchorage. We put on the deck lights and were amazed at the number of shell casings that littered the aft deck.

At the last moment, the *High Barbaree*, its engine overheating, and its crew shaken but relieved, sped into the bay and the green trawler continued steaming away to the north. We later surmised that they may have been waiting for darkness before making their move.

We anchored and squared away for the night. We left the generator running and kept the yacht well lit up. The crew from the other two yachts came aboard and we told them our tale. They also left their lights on, and one even moved nearer, so we were all close together. Upon inspecting the engine room, I found the main engine had boiled out most of its water and been close to burning itself up. We could not have carried on for much longer.

Tired as I was, I couldn't sleep, sitting on deck until the early hours of the morning. I had no idea how close those men on the trawler had come to ramming us, but I felt a little chill run down my spine as I considered what might have been. One thing for sure was that they had been deterred by our show of strength and our willingness to fight back. I know that everyone aboard the *High Barbaree* was scared that day, but I also know that if the drug pirates had tried to board our vessel, they would have had a real fight on their hands.

There is a satisfying end to this story. A few days later, we saw the green trawler again in the bight of Eleuthera. On this occasion, she was tied up alongside a large white U.S. Coast Guard cutter. We called them on the radio, but they wouldn't divulge much about the trawler, other than to say it was involved in illegal activities. They seemed preoccupied and not very interested in our story, which I found surprising, although we did find it difficult trying to relay all the details on the VHF.

We saw the trawler one last time on the television in Fort Lauderdale, when it was reported as being arrested with millions of dollars of drugs aboard and its Colombian crew being charged.

*

*Clifford, Lou, and Capt. Walter aboard Janeen.
A few minutes later I went for a swim.*

"OVERBOARD"

We all have exciting moments in life, and this was one of mine. We had just left port Castries bound for Martinique. I was forward trimming the headsails on my father's 138-foot schooner *Janeen* when a bight of jib sheet caught me about the waist, and I was airborne, and water bound!

Although the Caribbean Sea is warm, it feels icy cold, and I sink beneath the frothy surface. The saltwater stings my eyes as I open them, and I see the dark blurred form of the schooner's keel as it rushes away. I can't believe it, but I've gone overboard. My head breaks the surface and a wavelet goes down my throat choking me. Struggling to stay afloat I watch the schooner moving swiftly away.

"Help," I scream.

The skipper's head peers over the taffrail as he looks towards me. But it's as if he hasn't seen me. I try to wave, but it's difficult trying to tread water and wave at the same time. The mate's dark head appears then; he's throwing a life ring over. I remember my father's words of months before.

"When you see how long it takes to tack and get this big schooner around, you'll realize how long it would take for us to come back and try to pick you up if you fall in the drink. A bloody long time!"

The schooner grows smaller with incredible speed and finally the tips of her masts disappear beyond the crests of the waves. Suddenly, I am alone; there is only the sea. And then the life ring comes into view floating on a wave crest a few feet away. Swimming over I put the circle over my head placing both arms over the edges. The gold letters *Janeen* and Panama seem somehow ludicrous, but the float holds me, and I can at least rest for a moment.

The minutes go by, and I am still alone. Why don't they come back for me? I cannot see the schooner or even any land. The emptiness of the horizon causes me to doubt my sanity and I am overwhelmed by a feeling of absolute and utter aloneness. There can be no other situation where someone can feel such isolation. Panic strikes for a moment and beneath the sting of the salt water my eyes blur with tears. My head must appear very small in the rough water, like a floating coconut.

Looking around the horizon again and again, I realize that there is no reference, only the sea. Not knowing which way to look for the schooner, I spin continuously using my feet as paddles. The thought crosses my mind that this could be the end. They will not find me. Although it feels like an eternity, only twenty minutes have passed since I went into the water. I must not give up hope; if I can hold on for a while they will come back.

The *Janeen* appears then, on the top of a wave in the distance. They have shortened down to forestaysail and jumbo, and she is obviously under power, but my heart misses a beat. She's a half-mile to windward and not heading in my direction at all. I wave and scream until a generous dollop of saltwater goes down my throat causing me to choke and stop. Then she disappears again, headed away from me. They have not seen me.

The minutes wear on and the sun gradually rises in the sky. Glancing at my Seiko watch, I see that I have been swimming for more than 35 minutes. The watch is still working and in a moment of macabre humor I remember the salesman's pitch at the store where I had bought it.

"Waterproof down to 600 feet."

I am angered. Who cares if it is waterproof to a depth of 600 feet? The man has played a bad joke on me and in my frustration, I rip it from my wrist to fling it away. It sinks quickly and I take solace in the knowledge that it will soon pass the 600-foot mark. The *Janeen* has gone, and I am alone. Time passes, but the concept that they may not find me is still hard for me to accept. The horizon remains clear when I'm lifted to the crest of the waves, and I look desperately for any sign of the schooner. In the troughs I can see nothing, and it's as if I'm in a deep pit; I am trapped just as surely in my watery prison. The surface of the sea turns a gray green shade as clouds cover the sun.

Thirty feet from my face a large dark fin breaks the surface. I quickly put my head underwater and open my eyes. The salt stings, but against the dark blur of the ocean a vague dark gray form moves sinuously. The image is vague and poorly defined but there is no mistaking the ghostly form of a huge fish. My chest tightens as I lift my head to breathe; the fin is there, circling me. It is a foot above the water, and I imagine the curve as it joins the creature's back. There are many kinds of fear experienced by man but perhaps the most chilling is that of being eaten alive. I am stricken with a terror that renders my body rigid; I am helpless within the creature's realm. Long helpless seconds pass as almost imperceptibly he closes the circle. He and I are from different worlds and fate has brought us together in this strange meeting. Finally, he makes a lunge and moves directly towards me. The fin disappears below the surface. Holding my breath, I close my eyes and instinctively tuck my legs up beneath my body waiting for the savage impact that will surely come. The seconds go by, and I feel the rush of water beneath me. Daring to look again I see the huge form swim only a foot or two below me, and then the ethereal form disappears into the depths; It has gone; I feel relief. Was it a shark? I don't know. Perhaps it was a large dolphin or pilot whale. I think that it must be an omen. I feel reassured. If I had been meant to die the creature would have had me, I am certain of it, and then suddenly I see the *Janeen* again. She is coming straight towards me. There is no doubt this time, my shipmates are waving to me, and I can see their faces and hear shouts. I wave and scream back.

In a demonstration of excellent seamanship, the skipper brings the ship alongside and just to windward of me and the mate throws a heaving line. Within moments I am aboard.

As I stand on the deck waves of gratitude and relief come over me. I would never see life in the old way again.

"You're lucky Lou." the skipper tells me. We would have lost you at nightfall for sure."

My shipmates look at me with strange eyes. I am one who has returned from the very edge of death.

Esau Mack was a fine seaman as well as a great sea cook.

Fishes Alive

Thousands of small islands and cays make up the broad group of islands known as the Bahamas. All are flat low-lying coral-based landmasses, and the surrounding waters are filled with dangerous reefs. White sand beaches abound and in the early days there were few visitors to the out islands other than the local fishermen and the occasional charter yacht. The long island of Eleuthera offers good shelter to the west and we found ourselves there in the mid-sixties. After a charter through the Berry Islands to the north, we were headed back to the lower Caribbean and the captain stopped to see some friends at the small French Leave resort.

Bahamians eat a lot of seafood, and we tried many interesting island recipes. Conch, crayfish, giant whelks, sea urchin, and a wide variety of fish were readily available and usually for free if you could catch them yourself.

They say that behind every great recipe there's a great chef. Behind this particular fish dish, there's a funny "tail." I've sampled seafood around the world and most of the dishes were good. The Mediterranean bouillabaisse, Bahamian conch chowder, and the fresh dolphin head (dolphin fish, not the mammal) chowder of the Windward Islands are all favorites of mine. Whenever I make a fish chowder, I always rely on a recipe given to me by a great old seafaring cook named Esau Mack.

Esau was a jovial man from Antigua who served as cook on my father's schooner *Caribee* in the 1960s. He had sailed on many local vessels over the years and had been to most of the islands many times. He was a fine seaman in his own right and when the skipper called all hands to make sail, Esau would appear on deck in his dirty apron and could be counted on to know the difference between the peak jig and the boom tackle. His local knowledge of the reefs and bays of the islands was unsurpassed, and the captain wasn't above asking him for a bit of advice on occasion.

"I know all de reefs round dese cays, 'cause I been put on most of dem from time to time." he would chuckle.

Although his virtues as a seagoing cook were exceptional, he was possessed of three vices common to sailormen: rum, women, and gambling.

He was especially partial to the strong white mixture known locally as Jack Iron, an unlabeled brew that kicked like a mule. It was cheap and available in the little rum shops of every port. Although it was against the ship's rules, and despite the captain's best efforts, Esau usually managed to smuggle a bottle or two aboard. Hidden in the bottom of the vegetable basket below the breadfruit and bananas the Jack Iron would find its way to the *Caribee's* galley and Esau would imbibe the brew from time to time as the fancy took him.

Esau was a compulsive gambler and would not quit until he had exhausted all lines of credit. As for the women, there were always one or two local ladies with little ones on their hips waiting on the quay to pounce on poor Esau as soon as he stepped ashore, demanding a share of his pay.

He would try to hide below decks until the coast was clear, but as the cook he would inevitably have to go ashore to the local market for vegetables, where they would nab him then.

The West Indian crews on the schooners were big fish chowder fans too and it was customary for them to fish off the bow after the schooner was anchored for the night. Quite often, schools of small red snapper, jacks, or yellow tail would appear under the bowsprit, attracted by the glow of the anchor light. The deckhands would sit and yarn and as they pulled in fish they would pass them down through the galley hatch to Esau, who would clean them for the fish stew.

One evening, Esau was having more than a regular pull from the bottle of Jack Iron he kept hidden behind the spice rack. The water level in the fish pot rose and the first aromas began wafting up the galley air vent and along the deck, finally reaching the stern and the skipper's olfactory glands. He stopped what he was doing and made for the galley to investigate what culinary delights Esau was preparing.

He was immediately suspicious, as the sweet smell of Jack Iron rum became evident. Any question regarding the sobriety of the cook disappeared when the skipper peered into the large pot cooking on the stove. There amongst the onions and tomatoes a live jackfish swam around in circles.

Talk about fresh! That night's fish stew was cancelled, but Esau went on to prepare many more great ones.

Ramona sailing well with everything correctly set and the sails full. Shot from the Janeen's deck. We were racing these two beauties to train up their crews.

"Racing the Big Ones"

Who can say what draws us to the sea? Why do we feel uplifted as we stand on a headland facing the ocean? Perhaps it is the music of the wind and the waves as it carries to us. Perhaps it is the fact that life itself consists mainly of water. Or could it be something else? Could it be the beautiful form of a graceful schooner making her way westwards? Surely above all the spirit of man is moved by the sights and sound of a fine schooner at sea. The movement of her hull through the water must be the seaman's ballet. The sound of the wind filling her sails the sailor's aria, and the love that he feels for his ship is that of a man for a woman.

Perhaps more so than most, coastal seafaring folk feel this. There is a sense of the ocean there, to be sure. They are now and have always been a sea people, born to a legacy of great wind ships and strong adventurous men who loved and understood the ocean. Their forefathers built great wind ships and sailed them from coastal ports since the very beginning and even those who claim to be landsmen have an uncle, grandfather or distant cousin who went to sea from some seaport. Fine sailing ships were born here, and their heritage is just as surely steeped in the salty Atlantic as it is rooted in the soil of the land.

I left the east coast of Canada on one of my father's schooners when I was but one year old to live a life before the mast. As a young lad growing up in the West Indies, I was lucky to have a father who was in the cruise business. In fact, my father Capt. Walter Boudreau, was a pioneer in the industry and he, along with men like Lou Kennedy, and Commander V.E.B. Nicholson OBE, really started the whole thing after the Great War. They were able to buy large sailing yachts for a few thousand dollars and there seemed to be an endless supply of folks willing to pay to sail the unspoiled Caribbean on them.

At one time in the late sixties and early seventies, we owned two remarkable sailing vessels, *Ramona*, and *Le Voyageur*. Both were steel Herreshoff schooners built in 1918 and 1921, respectively. 138 feet overall, with 24-foot beam and about 15-foot draft, they each had an outside lead ballast keel of more than 50 tons. As well as being extremely luxurious, they were very fast. They had superb sailing qualities befitting their pedigree, both being weatherly and excellent in light airs. With a good deck gang, the two schooners handled very well and were not prone to loggy tacking, as some of their cousins were.

The *Ramona* made a record in the Transpacific race some years prior to our ownership and logged some 367 nautical miles in 24 hrs. The *Le Voyageur*, under her previous name *Mariette*, was the only schooner other than the famed *Bluenose* to beat the great American challenger *Gertrude L Thebaud* (1930). Much later, I was her captain for a time.

The two schooners, although 100% alike in hull shape, tonnage, rudder, and ballast, had different rigs. The *Ramona* was gaff-rigged and the *Le Voyageur* Marconi. *Ramona's* gaff rig was slightly larger in total square footage and her main was bigger. *Le Voyageur's* fisherman topsail which flew above the main staysail was much larger than the *Ramona's*. *Le Voyageur's* larger balloon jib was bigger as well than the *Ramona's* traditional jib topsail.

Every year before the start of the winter charter season the two schooners would be anchored at their home port of Marigot Bay, St. Lucia, and my father and Capt. Dressel would be selecting and training up their crews for the upcoming season. This involved several training days up and down the coast and what better way to put a shine on a new gang than to let them race, and that we did.

Dawn saw us up and getting ready for sea, laying out the running rigging and hoisting boats. We took the ties out of the topsails and put twine stops in the fisherman. Close all portholes and then the two skippers would give the order to heave anchor with a small circular motion of their fingers.

The *Ramona* and *Le Voyageur* would heave anchor early in the morning and round up to set sail in the lee of the island. They were an awesome sight, these tall-sparred ocean Valkyries sailing close hauled under full sail to the north and then running downwind to the west of the island. I was lucky enough to sail on both schooners over the training periods and the thrill of those balmy island days with two of the finest schooners ever to grace the water doing battle before the brisk trade winds is indelibly etched in my mind.

We raced the two schooners several times to the west of St. Lucia and into the Martinique channel. We compared them on all points as well, running off, reaching, and close hauled. Although the results were slightly in *Ramona's* favor, the schooners were a close match indeed, with neither the *Ramona* nor *Le Voyageur* ever taking a big lead. The gaff rigged *Ramona* clearly did better on any point reaching or off the wind while the Marconi rigged *Le Voyageur* seemed to point a bit higher and was able to hold her speed a little closer to the wind. My recollection is that the gaff-rigged *Ramona* was slightly ahead most of the time.

The surprise came when the skippers changed ships one day. My father who had been sailing the *Ramona* took *Le Voyageur* and gave *Ramona* to the younger Joel Dressel who had been sailing *Le Voyageur*. *Le Voyageur* did better on that day. It was clear that the performance of two closely matched schooners depended on the skill and experience of the skipper.

Although I could not have realized it back then, it was the only time that these two lovely Nathanael Greene Herreshoff sisters would ever test each other in the warm waters of the West Indies. I was truly a fortunate young fellow to have been part of it.

We leave a squall astern with upper canvas on deck and a reefed main.

A Voyage on the Schooner Janeen

Logbook October 1968

Departed Miami, Florida, bound for St. Lucia in the Eastern Caribbean

This may have been one of my earliest memories of a voyage on the Mariette. My father owned and captained the schooner then and following a refit in Florida we were bound south for a winter charter season. She was at that time called Janeen after my sister. We left Miami in mid-October, and after rounding the Berry Islands and Spanish Wells we sailed into the Atlantic. But now I will let my old logbook speak for itself.

The smells of the land have faded and now there is just the sea. The odor of pine trees and damp earth is gone, replaced by the crisp aroma of deep blue ocean. We have left the world of mortal men behind us, transcending into that of the North Atlantic Schooner man. Far from land, our speeding schooner rolls gently, dipping her lee rail before surging on. She is in her element; a white-winged sea spirit dancing to a tune only the sailor man knows. The ocean catches her lee turnbuckles in a rush of spray before she lifts, and above her decks tall spars carry a press of taught canvas.

Well-trimmed jibs and forestaysail power her onwards even as the main and jib topsails pull her ever faster. Stay sheets and halyards strain to hold their willful charges and as I tilt my head slightly, I can hear her wooden spars moan and laugh in the language of the deep-sea schooner. Occasionally, when she takes a deep roll, the end of her long main boom tastes the sea, rending it with a quickly healing wound. Her long black hull leaves a frothy wake astern, even as her perfect symmetry of sail glides serenely above the turbulent ocean like some graceful white-winged seabird.

In the morning sunlight the droplets of ocean coming over the rail glisten like so many flying diamonds before reaching my face. The feel of the salt spray is invigorating and as I lick the salt from around my mouth, I savor the taste. We seem almost inconsequential on the empty expanse of the great ocean and as I scan the horizon, we appear to be alone. But we are not. Sea birds accompany us on our way; small dark petrels dive and disappear between the troughs of the waves, fluttering madly to keep up with us. They seem happy, almost playful, and not in the least concerned about their seemingly isolated location. Dolphins come to play under our bow, but they stay only a short while; perhaps we're too fast. They leap and frolic just under the bowsprit netting and as they turn sideways looking upward, I can see an intelligence there. They click at me, and I whistle back. They hear me; there's someone home. Their streamlined silvery gray bodies seem to move effortlessly through the water and when they breach for a quick breath we can hear the whoosh-pop as they exhale and breathe in.

The deep-sea routine is traditional and time-honored. The cook serves three squares a day and while the fare is simple the crew wolf it down without complaint. The schooner needs constant care, and we attend to our duties as the hours pass. The mate adds another piece of baggy wrinkle to the foremast aft lower shroud while the boson cobbles up a start in the jumbo clew before it opens further. We stand our wheel watches trying our best to keep the fast-moving vessel on her course. Inevitably someone strays and the mate is there in a second.

"Keep her steady, there." My father the skipper growls.

He raises his sextant at noon and by some method known only to him he places our latitude. He checks the rig and trim every watch and if need be he orders a pull here, or a foot slacked off there.

"Take a couple feet on the main here." He called to Jack the mate.

Evening comes and the ship's bell rings in the turn of the watch. As the sun sinks in the west a cloak of darkness covers the schooner, but she rolls on, uncaring of the change. For her, the ocean remains infinite, and her purpose on it unchanged. For us, however, there is magic; the aura of the ocean night casts a spell on the schooner that is very special. Standing our watches through the darkness the eerie glows of the port and starboard lights throw ghostly color into the salt spray as it rises from the bow. Like an endless kaleidoscope show, sudden flashes of red, then green, then darkness again.

Just forward of the wheel the red-tinted binnacle light turns the helmsman's face into a bizarre demon-like visage and the glow of the lookout's cigarette stands out like a tiny red beacon in the night. The schooner feels more alive than ever during the hours of darkness. Perhaps because we can no longer see her, we more consciously feel her. She lifts her stem gently, reaping the night wind and then heeling slightly, she takes sustenance from it before rolling on. Under the lee bow a wave of white water rises, higher even than the rail, but as the schooner surges forward, it curves away to fall on the dark Atlantic, rolling away to leeward with an angry hiss. White water races away from the lee rail in almost magical form before disappearing into nothingness. The zone of blackness ends as I glance aloft. There, the tips of her masts trace a meandering course through an endless sea of stars.

Morning comes and the skipper sits on the stern with a mug to savour the sunrise. My father has conquered the ocean before.

Log schooner Janeen

Position 280 miles east northeast of the Turks and Caicos, wind 25 knots.

Coming on deck again the skipper gives us a change of course.

"Come 10 degrees to starboard." he says, and we carefully spoke the helm a little to starboard.

Even though it is only a small course change the schooner feels it right away. It has brought the angle of the wind a little more ahead.

"Don't bother to trim Jack." the skipper says, "We'll try a few miles at a time to the east until we get the wind we want."

And so, we alter course towards the east to get a better slant. But as morning progresses it doesn't take long before the wind increases, gusting over 30 knots. Long feeder bands of vicious squalls begin to swing in from the northeast and soon the black line on the horizon will be upon us. It will bring wind, plenty of wind, but the *Janeen* is fine for the moment.

Everyone gathers in the helm area. We huddle behind the spray guard looking miserable. I look down at my own hands. They hold the brass guardrail surrounding the helm in a vice-like grip. My knuckles are white. For the first time since I've been aboard the *Janeen*, I am afraid. The adolescent thrill at seeing this big schooner pushed to the limit has long gone. But my father knows.

Towards noon the first feeder band hits and the schooner trembles like a thing alive and she is. The big main sheet pops and crackles with the new strain. It takes up the last fractional millimeter of slack in the knot making it fast to the bit and we feel it thorough the deck. Every piece of cordage on the vessel creaks and stretches to the limit. The air whines and hums in the rigging. The shrouds make a whistling sound like wailing banshees and the wind comes on stronger. The dark squall clouds rush overhead, and Matt and I are called to the wheel again. It is even more difficult to hold her now and we struggle to keep the course.

"Bring her back to 295." the skipper shouts over the wind and we strain to haul the spokes back to leeward.

I stand near the skipper. The *Janeen* has a heavy weather helm now and we can't handle more than half an hour on the wheel; she is too demanding. My arms feel like lead, it will be a long 24 hours. The 10 degrees off the wind eases her but it's unnoticeable. The *Janeen* is on a wild run and there is no holding her back. The schooner makes many sounds now; below, her steel hull acts like an amplifier humming and groaning, and she makes strange cracking popping noises. There is a high-pitched whine where the water rushes over the feathered propellers. In the main salon the big wooden mainmast is making a sound like muffled thunder. It vibrates and shakes like a tree in a storm.

The hull portholes are continuously below the water now; she's well-heeled over. I look down through the inch-thick glass into the grey dark world below the surface of the sea towards the bottom of the Atlantic Ocean 1,000 fathoms down. The *Janeen* has never sailed like this. The knot meter doesn't fall below 14 knots now and when she surges in the gusts coming off the crests of the waves, she surfs at 16. Every fiber of the heavy Dacron sailcloth is stretched to the very limit. The sails are bellied out, and the booms and gaffs are bent like bows under the strain. The whole rig creaks and groans over the screech of the wind. The wire shrouds and stays whine like guitar strings and she flies on. Under her bow a 20-foot curve of white water shears off to leeward and astern she is leaving a wake like a destroyer.

Our schooner lifts and surges ahead, putting her cheek to the next wave. The wall of water shears off her bow again and she leans over so far that we must hold tight to something or go over. Occasionally a big wave hits her steel hull square on, and it is as if a giant hammer has hit us. The frightening "Cath-ump" sound shakes her from keel to topmast and the spray rises halfway to the crosstrees before flying over us.

We fly on through the blackness of the night until the first hint of daylight appears to the east. I have never sailed like this. Maybe no one has. And then it is morning again and St Lucia lies ahead over the horizon in the Windward Islands The schooner has run like the wind. But now we rest.

Logbook schooner Janeen

Marigot Bay, St Lucia

Under a moonlit sky the schooner rests in Marigot's inner lagoon, swinging gently at her anchor in three fathoms of water. There is a sandy bottom, and the big fisherman hook lies with one fluke buried.

That evening there is a welcome party in the wardroom for the charter agents. Humboldt the steward serves drinks while Pierre serves his canapés. The Yacht Haven Hotel charter folks arrive with other important people, to see us and our schooner. There's a woman with a huge pompadour and men in their blue yachting blazers.

"Did you have a nice sail?" she asks me, "Oh yes, and thank you," I reply.

"Do you ever put all the sails up?"

How could they know? A 17-year-old deckhand on a classic schooner flying through the darkness with two of us at the helm trying to hold her. The shrieking wind and schooner trembling and shaking as the knot meter passes sixteen.

I smile dutifully.

"Yes, we do ma'am."

A giant pink snail crawls up the beach near our house in Marigot Bay, St. Lucia.

The Giant Pink Snail

Sailors all over world seem to experience the strange and unexplainable. We have heard of the Flying Dutchman doomed forever to sail the oceans denied for eternity a safe harbor. And the Bermuda triangle where ships and people have apparently disappeared. And this Cape Breton sea captain has seen some pretty strange things as well. Muffin, the great white shark was only the most recent strange tale I have told. I have been accused of stretching the truth, but I assure you that this is a fact as true as can be.

So brave reader, listen to this tale I will tell. Its veracity is without doubt as documented by the photograph, and as I sit here in Nova Scotia today some 50 years later, I can still remember our encounter with a strange sea creature and holding on to the shell of that giant beast as it gave us a ride across the bay.

Many years ago, my family left the fair pine treed coast of Nova Scotia to live in the West Indies. In St. Lucia, where I grew up there was an occurrence that is indeed hard to believe. Our home was in a beautiful landlocked lagoon called Marigot Bay, where my father, a famous Nova Scotia sea captain ran schooners.

Early one morning, there was a shout that there was something on the beach. Indeed, as I looked out onto the sandy beach, I could not believe my eyes, but there it was, a giant pink snail on the beach. My siblings and I lost no time in running as fast as we could down the shore towards the creature. Someone got a camera and took a picture of it.

Sure enough, as we approached, it turned its giant head slightly to gaze down at us. It had large eyes and two small antennae coming off the top of its head. It made a loud growling kind of noise as it came out and slowly made its way up the beach and stopped. My siblings and I, being rather brave, even went as far as touching it. The skin was thick and rubbery with shells and bits of weed hanging from it.

After a short while a strangely dressed gentleman with a top hat came by, wondering aloud about the health of the snail. It allowed him to put a ladder in front of its head. The snail seemed to know what was coming next. The man then climbed the ladder with a large bucket of purple Kool-Aid which he poured down the snail's throat. He smiled saying that it was a medicinal concoction and that he had just fed the snail something that would make it better.

That we were in any way witness to something strange or untoward never occurred to us. We were just some Canadian kids growing up in the West Indies, who just happened to find a giant snail in front of their house.

Later that day, the man beckoned us to climb up upon the snail's back, where it met the shell telling us that the snail would be happy to give us a ride. We looked at this as a wonderful opportunity and climbed up there and took a seat. We were thrilled to say the least. How many kids can claim that they rode the back of a giant snail when they were ten years old?

So, if there are any who doubt still that Cape Breton schooner Captains have strange experiences growing up, please take this as proof otherwise. Giant pink snails that drink purple Kool-Aid do exist and they give rides to Canadian kids.

Bupa roams her home between the Pitons in St. Lucia, Windward islands.

BUPA THE ELEPHANT

Jalousie Bay on the southwestern end of St. Lucia is probably the most awe-inspiring anchorage in the Windward Islands, and I always enjoyed taking my charter guests there to share the majesty and beauty of this pristine spot. Gross and Petit Pitons rose precipitously from the blue Caribbean, rugged volcanic cones that had been forced upwards eons ago by unknown titanic forces. The tiny anchorage of Jalousie lay between these twin peaks and a peaceful lush green valley studded with coconut trees led inland to a jungle cull de sac. The water was extremely deep there, and we had to drop the hook very close to shore to find bottom.

We often put a stern line ashore to the coconut trees to stop us from swinging. When we looked upwards it always seemed as though the towering Petit Piton was hanging over our vessel. I have never seen a more beautiful sight than the full moon rising into a clear sky between the Pitons.

In the eighties, a wealthy British entrepreneur came to St. Lucia with a grandiose plan. In previous years he had played a large part in developing the island of Mustique for the rich and famous and he was well-known in high circles. He bought the lush valley between the beautiful Pitons where he planned to build some kind of African Garden of Eden. There would be a main Krall surrounded by rondavel huts, air conditioned of course, and he would populate his valley with African animals. But, for some reason his plans went astray, and the project came to a halt while still in the planning stages. There was one innocent player however, who suffered badly from this scheme, Bupa the elephant.

Now Bupa, was a real African elephant, a little one to be sure but the genuine article. She had been only a few years old when she was taken from her native land, transported to St. Lucia, and let loose in the Jalousie valley. She was to have been the first of the animals to inhabit the beautiful valley, but Bupa turned out to be the only one. It was sad in a way, to see this wild African animal, intelligent and of a gregarious nature, taken by man and placed in a lush prison. She would grow up alone, never again to enjoy the company of her own kind.

Yachts visiting this most beautiful of anchorages would see the rapidly growing elephant wandering the grass between the coconut trees of the valley, chasing chickens with her trunk, and occasionally smacking the small pig who enjoyed antagonizing her. She became quite the tourist attraction and the yachtsmen who tied up with stern lines to the coconut trees had great fun feeding and playing with Bupa. She quickly recognized the yachts as a ready food source and would come down to the shore in the early morning begging. She liked bread and could easily handle a couple of loaves at a time. Years passed and she grew. Soon she was towering a good eight feet above the ground.

I often sailed the *High Barbaree* to Jalousie on our charter cruises during those years and we made friends with Bupa. Purchasing a bucket of local fruit from the young vendors who came out in their row boats, we would take the dinghy ashore to the beach. Seeing us land, Bupa would trot towards the water's edge with her trunk extended in front of her, smelling the air. She had the most fascinating long eyelashes and bright shiny eyes. With her trunk she would smell the fruit and we would begin to feed her. It was a bit cheeky, but we found that as long as you were feeding Bupa, she would stand still and let posers climb to her back for a picture. But when we were down to the last mango or papaya the rider would be told to dismount. We had learned that as soon as the food was gone Bupa would endeavor to rid herself of the person on her back. It was quid pro quo.

There were many stories told of "Bupa the African elephant of Jalousie," but one I remember better than the rest. The Moorings charter company was operating their fleet of bareboats from Marigot Bay then, and one of their groups consisted of six vacationing doctors. After leaving Marigot at noon on the first day of their cruise, they decided to stop in Jalousie for the night. In the waning evening light, they dropped a bow anchor while one of the local fishermen took a stern line ashore to the coconut trees. By the time they had secured their yacht for the night it was dark, and the doctors turned to more important matters.

A bottle of the fine Mount Gay rum was broached, and the vacationers sat in the cockpit savoring the sounds of the tropical night and the beauty of the moon rising between the Pitons. Through a haze of rum swizzle, the men missed the occasional trumpeting of an African elephant. By the time the last of the sailors took sleep their second bottle of Mount Gay had suffered serious damage. They slept soundly till dawn.

The first of the doctors awoke as the sun began to peak above the ridge to the east of Jalousie valley. He lay in bed for a moment before noticing a strange motion on the sloop. It seemed to be swaying and surging fore and aft, but there was no swell. Perhaps he thought, they had dragged their anchor during the night. He rolled groggily from his bunk and called to his nearest friend and donning the light blue hospital jammies that they wore they came on deck.

Through bleary eyes they saw a large African elephant with their stern line in its trunk Bupa was pulling the small sloop back and forth. The men looked shoreward with disbelief before calling their comrades from below. The story is told that the good doctors abstained from the rum for the balance of their voyage. Pink elephants indeed!

And then she was gone. The following season I sailed into Jalousie and dropped my anchor as usual, and the local lads rowed out to us with their baskets of fruit and fresh fish to sell.

"I'll take a bucket of mangoes for Bupa." I asked in the usual way, but they looked at me in a puzzled fashion.

"Eh, eh, you don't know? Bupa de elephant dead."

"Dead? What do you mean?" I asked.

"Somebody did poison her, you know."

I later heard rumors of a vengeful caretaker who was mauled by the elephant, but I will always remember gentle Bupa the African elephant who took fruit from my hand and playfully pulled my hair with her trunk.

Cleopatra's Barge II.
Built in 1915, she is still sailing and winning races today.

CLEOPATRA'S BARGE II

Back in the year 1918 in a place called Bristol, Rhode Island, a beautiful schooner was launched at the Herreshoff shipyard. She was the creation of a brilliant designer by the name of Nathanael Greene Herreshoff, also known as the wizard of Bristol. She was steel plated with high grade plate and riveted with outside lead ballast. It was clear after sea trials that she was destined to be fast. She had been originally commissioned as Mariette by John Jacob Brown of Boston, Massachusetts, head of a well-known wealthy family of the day. Some years later another Massachusetts family named Crowninshield bought her and renamed her Cleopatra's Barge II. A previous generation of this family had built and launched another vessel that was known as Americas first yacht and named her Cleopatra's Barge.

I am in possession of a logbook chronicling the exploits of the *Cleopatra's Barge II* under the ownership of Francis B Crowninshield.

Some people of the day called the logbook the social register of Massachusetts on account of the many socialites who graced the Barge's decks for an evening cocktail or two and if they were lucky a sail aboard.

The 1930's were the era of the famous international fisherman's schooner races where swift American schooners tested themselves against the fine Nova Scotians and in particular the schooner *Bluenose* of Lunenburg under the command of Captain Angus Walters.

The *Bluenose* had gained a reputation as being unbeatable in the races and took on all the excellent U.S. challengers off Lunenburg or Gloucester.

The best of the U.S. schooners one year was a fine vessel named the *Gertrude L Thebaud*. The *Thebaud* under the command of Captain Ben Pine defeated all her American sisters and came to be known as the champion of the U.S. schooner fishing fleet.

And so it came to pass that in 1931 the *Bluenose* raced the *Thebaud* in the international fisherman schooner races. Capt. Walters spent many days off Lunenburg tuning the ship and crew to be in top racing trim. Capt. Ben Pine and the *Thebaud* did the same off Gloucester.

Meanwhile the *Cleopatra's Barge II* continued her pleasure sailing off Gloucester under the command of Captain Charles Lawson. One day in October 1931, the *Thebaud* saw the *Barge* off Gloucester and in an unofficial test of speed endeavored to sail by her in a breeze of wind. This did not bode well for Captain Ben Pine and the *Thebaud* as they were soundly beaten by the *Barge*. The following day October 31, 1931, the day was calm off Gloucester with little wind. Captain Pine spotted the *Barge* again and lowering a dory rowed over and came alongside her. Captain Ben Pine met Captain Lawson at the rail of the *Barge* and challenged him to an official race the following day around the fisherman's triangular racecourse. After a brief consultation with his boss Mr. Crowninshield, he agreed. And so, it was recorded in the logbook of the *Cleopatra's Barge II*, that they met the *Thebaud* off Marblehead in an official test of speed around the fisherman's schooner racecourse. It was Thursday October 2, 1931. Mr. Crowninshield had intended to haul down his end of season flags the previous morning, but he changed his mind to go over the course racing against *Gertrude L Thebaud*. At 9:00 a.m., Francis Crowninshield, Emily Davis, Lewis Bacon, Commodore Sears, and Gordon Dexter came aboard for the race. The wind was brisk from the northeast, so they took the launch and longboat on deck. They beat to eastern point and there they met the *Thebaud* coming out of Gloucester. The *Barge* took her on over the fisherman's course.

From the log of Cleopatra's Barge II

"It was a triangle course five miles to a leg. Taking the windward one first we let her start ahead by 45 seconds and the *Thebaud* led the *Barge* all the way almost to the first mark. We had our chance after that, and the *Barge* took the lead just before rounding the windward mark and added another minute on the downwind leg. On the last leg of the course, we steadily increased our lead and crossed the line at least three minutes before the *Thebaud*. It was a fine ending to a fine sailing season and another grand day out on the water. Shortly afterwards we put the launch in the water and as we did so, the flags came down in

CLEOPATRA'S BARGE II

1931. "I might be excused by my remark that I hated to see them come down." – Francis B Crowninshield"

The *Thebaud* could not hold the Herreshoff schooner and Captain Ben Pine was sent home defeated. Later he tried his best in the fisherman's schooner races again but captain Ben Pine of the *Thebaud* could not best the great Nova Scotian *Bluenose* and he sadly realized that his lovely schooner would never win against the *Bluenose*.

Jump forward to the present year 2022. This fine schooner is still sailing. Several years ago, the *Mariette* as the *Cleopatra's Barge II* had been originally named, raced across the Atlantic Ocean to celebrate her 100th birthday. I wrote an earlier book "*The Man Who Loved Schooners,*" and mentions that *Mariette* had been sailing under Boudreau family ownership and was called the *Janeen* after captain Walter's oldest daughter. It also came to pass that the owners eldest son Captain Lou was in command of the schooner for a time as well. Today, this Nova Scotian sea captain who had been in command of *Janeen*, the only schooner other than the *Bluenose* to beat the *Gertrude L Thebaud*, lives on the south shore of Nova Scotia. As part of my seagoing career I also sailed on *Bluenose II* as a deckhand.

My family first bought the schooner *Mariette* in the early 50s from a woman in Oyster Bay, New York. She kept the schooner at the dock all year with her tall spars hidden in a big shed. She had her crew step the masts and rig it up for a couple of weeks sailing around her birthday after which the schooner was put away again until the following year and her next birthday. My father sailed her in his charter business for several years including at least two transatlantic voyages. Later the Boudreau family bought her sister ship called *Ramona* and we became the only family to own these identical twins. Later on, the *Janeen* was sold to the owner of Almaden Vineyards, a vintner in California. Sadly, some years later the *Ramona* was lost in a storm north of Bermuda under the command of Captain Ross McKay.

Our family was lucky enough to be able to purchase *Janeen* a second time from the United States Navy where she was used as a training ship. We put a crew aboard her at Coco Solo naval base in Panama.

VENUS OF DOMINICA

Our charter cruises often took us to the beautiful island of Dominica in the Windward Islands. Wild and primitive, her lush green mountains rose precipitously from the sea, while deep jagged ravines ran inland from bays and coves with black volcanic sand beaches. Of all the Windward Islands, Dominica, with its verdant jungle, was perhaps the most naturally stunning.

The village of Portsmouth is situated at the north end of the island in Prince Rupert Bay, a large natural harbor giving superb shelter in most weather conditions. A long sandy beach lined with coconut trees ran from the colorfully painted houses and shops of the town to a heavily treed bluff to the north.

Nestled in the rugged mountains above the village, a lush green valley held the only remaining enclave of Carib Indians. At the time, these were perhaps the last living remnants of the once war-like tribe that had once ruled the islands of the eastern Caribbean. A company called "Dominica Safaris" began operations that year using zebra striped Land Rovers, with drivers dressed in bush jackets and safari hats. They drove tourists into the remote mountainous center of the island to visit jungle waterfalls and old plantations, the high point being a visit to the Carib Indian reservation in the north.

The Jungle River runs inland from Portsmouth town, and we often ferried our guests there to see the many species of exotic birds and dense tropical rain forest lining the banks.

In January 1973, we anchored the *Janeen* in Portsmouth, and that night we had the good fortune to see the remarkable "Venus," at the "Spotlight," the only entertainment establishment there at the time.

Within a few minutes of the anchor hitting the bottom, a fleet of little row boats, manned by young local lads, came out to us with fresh fish, vegetables, straw hats, and various handicrafts. Some offered coral jewelry and turtle shells, while others had conch and live lobsters. This floating carousel market circled around us, eager to sell their wares.

One rowboat, slightly larger than the others, came alongside with a very distinguished looking gentleman sitting at the stern. He introduced himself as Mr. Lamb (he pronounced it "Lumb"), the owner and operator of the "Spotlight" restaurant.

When he had gained the attention of a few of our guests and crew, Mr. Lamb launched into a well-rehearsed and animated pitch.

"Come to the Spotlight restaurant tonight. We have everything; steel band, limbo dance, Venus – the belly bottle dancer, and Bah-B-Q mountain chicken." he said smiling and waving his arms.

He caught everyone's attention with the bit about Venus the belly bottle dancer, and we leaned further over the rail to find out more.

"What does this Venus dancer do then?" one of our passengers asked.

Mr. Lamb, obviously enjoying himself, offered a more detailed explanation of his exclusive featured performer and her main act.

"She does the belly dance, de limbo dance, and den she does mash up all de empty bottles in the restaurant, and do thee bottle dance upon the broken glass." he finished emphatically.

This brought a few guffaws from guests and crew alike. It sounded as though Mr. Lamb was a con artist trying to lure clients into his restaurant.

"Doan laugh, what I say is true." he said in earnest. The host of our charter party turned to my father in amazement. "You mean she dances on broken glass, Skipper?"

"I guess. Do you want to go in and find out?" he replied just as curious as the host. So, seats were booked at the "Spotlight" restaurant for the show and Bar-B-Q dinner.

Generally, the crew were not allowed ashore during charters, but an exception was made this time, so that my father, my brother, myself, and a couple of others could witness this marvelous event. The crew gassed up the launch and cleaned it out in preparation for the evening's ferry service.

At seven o'clock, we made our run to the beach in front of the "Spotlight." It was calm and we put the bow to the shore. Mr. Lamb had the area lit up with kerosene torches and the steel band was already pinging away. The "Spotlight" was right on the water's edge and built of woven coconut palm siding, with a thatched roof held up by bamboo poles. Tables and chairs of roughly sawn local cedar timber stood awkwardly in the sand, surrounding a twenty-foot cement dance floor in the center.

The party was seated and rum punches with hibiscus flowers popping out of each glass were served. The evening menu was delightfully simple. You could choose rum punch or Carib beer, and either mountain chicken with breadfruit, or mountain chicken with rice and vegetables. Our guests chose the rice version. Mr. Lamb then told us he had once visited America and been to a seafood restaurant where you could choose your own live lobster straight out of a tank. He was so impressed by this, that he installed his own program along the same lines.

"Yeah man, you can choose you own mountain chickens." he said proudly ushering our passengers towards the back.

We followed him behind the bar where, in a dimly lit corner, stood a grotty chicken wire cage inhabited by dozens of huge frogs.

"Wait a minute, you said you were serving chicken?" my father asked slightly taken aback.

"Yes, but this is the famous Dominica mountain chicken, a real delicacy." Mr. Lamb said, equally taken aback that we did not immediately recognize his supposedly famous dish.

Going to the corner he picked up two broomsticks, with three-inch nails bound tightly to the ends, and smiling expansively he handed them to two of our men.

"You got to jook the frogs you want to eat and give them to me."

We watched in amusement as they engaged in this bizarre activity. The men tried to spear the big frogs through the mesh, and whenever they managed to jab one Mr. Lamb politely removed it from the end of the stick and took it away to be cooked. The ladies in the group emphatically declined, saying they would leave the spearing of the frogs to the "boys."

The "boys" found it wasn't as easy as it looked. The agile frogs were definitely not about to sit around and get skewered, and they hopped around making loud "rib-bit" noises, spiritedly avoiding the deadly stick.

The men worked up quite a sweat as they jabbed away, doing double-duty to catch ones for their wives. They eventually prevailed over the fast-moving frogs in the end and returned to their seats.

As the rum took effect, no one seemed to bother much about the swarms of biting mosquitoes buzzing about and our guests sat at their table and waited for the waitresses to bring their mountain chicken. The frog legs were fried and tasted just like small chicken drumsticks. The steel band banged away, and we were all beginning to get a little impatient, when Mr. Lamb finally announced that the show was about to begin.

The long-awaited Venus finally appeared on the stage, amidst a fanfare of whistles and clapping hands. She was a beautifully shaped young woman attired in a very skimpy bikini. She had hundreds of sparkling sequins on her bikini, as well as in her short black hair, and her gold capped teeth sparkled when she smiled.

Venus began dancing around the small concrete floor, while two assistants brought out a flaming limbo stick. With the encouragement of the audience, she managed to navigate this at an impossibly low level. After this, she jumped to the sandy floor searching the audience for an unsuspecting helper. My brother and I managed to leap behind the bamboo partition just in time. We watched from this position as Venus pounced on one of our unfortunate charter guests and dragged him to the dance floor, where she gyrated seductively, much to his embarrassment. The other men found this tremendously amusing, but the wives weren't looking any too happy and glared venomously at Venus.

Finally, the steel band slowed to a steady beat and Venus's two assistants placed a white canvas on the dance floor. They then made a round of the restaurant with two cardboard boxes, collecting the empty beer, rum, and wine bottles that had been consumed during the evening (which amounted to quite a few).

As we looked on in amazement, they broke the bottles into a deadly mass of jagged edges and swept them to the center of the stage. The jagged glass could clearly be seen from where we were sitting and there was no evidence of concealment or chicanery on anyone's part.

The steel band picked up momentum again and without warning, Venus suddenly jumped barefoot onto the glass. There was a cry of horror from everyone, even though this had been somewhat expected. The band beat a lively rhythm and Venus danced away. Her feet stomped up and down in the glass and she wiggled and squirmed while clapping her hands. There was no hesitation on her part, and she seemed to be enjoying it, smiling and laughing all the while.

She put a wooden chair on the stage and stood on it before leaping down into the glass again without sustaining a single cut, that we could tell.

She then made her most audacious move. Her two assistants were strong looking men of good stature and probably weighed a bit. Venus laid down in the broken glass and writhed around while one of the assistants stood on her stomach. He was a sensible fellow and wore his shoes.

To this day, I don't know how Venus managed her act without being horribly injured. After the show, she went from table to table displaying her smooth unblemished skin to all. Some of us went to check the glass as they were cleaning it up, only to find it was real enough.

As the years went by and we continued to sail the Windward Islands, I took many people to the "Spotlight" restaurant in Portsmouth, and we were always amazed by the bottle dance. Later, Mr. Lamb's place unfortunately burned down, and we never saw him again. No one in the islands ever heard what happened to the mysterious Venus or where she went, but she certainly had an unusual talent. We are still baffled, but there are some things in life that just can't be explained.

Two of the Boudreau fleet in Castries harbor where the hired skipper rammed the Janeen into the island trader Michael David at the north wharf.

LORDY LARDY

It was 1971 when my father was on the lookout for a responsible mariner to help him sail the 130-foot schooner, Le Voyageur. Chartering was a full-time job, and he was finding himself increasingly involved with the small hotel he had built in Marigot Bay. So, whenever a capable seafarer came by, he would offer them a job. I was home then, enjoying a period of leave following my service on the Bluenose II.

The *Le Voyageur* was a beautiful vessel and a living piece of American yachting history. She had once sailed under the name *Cleopatra's Barge II* owned by the Crowninshield family of Salem, Massachusetts, ship owners who played an important part in the early development of the shipping business in the U.S.

Cleopatra's Barge II was designed by the famous "Wizard of Bristol." Nat Herreshoff, at his shipyard in Bristol, Rhode Island. She was a fast sailing vessel and the only schooner on record, other than the *Bluenose*, to have beaten the famous American schooner *Gertrude L. Thebaud*. She did this in October 1931, just off Gloucester. She still sails today under the name *Mariette*.

Buster Grant was a fleet air arm pilot, taking a long leave of absence from the Royal Navy. Along with his wife and daughter, they had sailed across the Atlantic on their forty-foot catamaran. They ended up in Marigot Bay, where Buster began looking for some sort of employment to help with his cruising expenses. He was a short man with a Van Dyke beard and seemed to be of sound character. Dad hired him as mate of the two-hundred-ton *Le Voyageur*, in the hopes that he could train him as skipper.

Buster learned fast and before long he was acting as skipper, with Dad still aboard to keep an eye on him. A few weeks later, my father decided that Buster was ready to take command of the schooner by himself and he spoke to the new captain on the hotel patio.

"Buster," he said, "I am going to put you in command of the *Le Voyageur* now. The first thing I want you to do is to take her up to Castries harbor and go alongside the north wharf for fuel and water. Now remember, this vessel is a lot bigger and heavier to handle than your catamaran, so be careful."

Buster promised the skipper he wouldn't disappoint him. The two men shook hands and Buster strode off, his back straight and head high. We watched as Jongue, the mate, ferried the new skipper out to the anchored schooner. Buster immediately walked aft to the helm and rang the brass engine room telegraph to "stand by." After a moment, we heard the low rumble of the main engines as they started. Buster called Jongue to the wheel to discuss their imminent departure.

"Right Mr. Jongue, are we all ready to get under way?" he asked in his best Royal Navy voice.

"Yes, skipper, we're all set. The launch is up, and everything is ready on deck."

"Right then, you can heave up," Captain Buster ordered.

Jongue started the anchor winch, pulling the big stud link chain slowly over the wildcat. The winch was very powerful; it clinked and clanked and disappeared down the hawsepipe into the chain locker where "Chicken Back," the lowest ranking member of the crew, was busy stowing the chain. Finally, the anchor came up and was catted at the rail.

Buster's confidence grew by the minute. The engine room telegraphs jangled merrily as he rang "slow ahead," then "slow astern," and then "half ahead" to take the ship out of the bay.

Dad and I watched as the schooner's tall spars rounded the point and disappeared. Dad decided that we would both drive up to Castries to see how Buster handled his first docking maneuver.

The mate later filled us in on what subsequently took place. Once clear of Marigot's north point, Buster rang up "full ahead" and the twin diesel engines built up rpm until the schooner was forging north along the coast of St. Lucia towards Castries at ten knots. Buster put a helmsman at the wheel and strutted about the deck like a little admiral, proud of his new command.

As they neared the entrance to Castries harbor, the rest of the crew went about preparing the dock lines and cables for going alongside.

There were bow and stern lines, two spring lines, and two breast lines. Heaving lines were tied to the warps and heavy woven rope fenders hung over the side to protect the schooner's hull from the rough timbers of the commercial dock.

When they were abeam of Castries, Buster took the wheel from the deckhand and he brought the *Le Voyageur* to starboard, lining her up on the leading markers by which they would enter the harbor.

Meanwhile, Dad and I had arrived in town just in time to see the *Le Voyageur* round Tapion Rocks at the mouth of the harbor. We stood on the commercial dock with our binoculars watching as the schooner came into Castries harbor at full speed. She was moving fast with a white bone in her teeth.

Laying alongside the commercial wharf were two island trading schooners, the *Michael David* and the *Granvelass*. These schooners carried a wide variety of cargo from island to island in the eastern Caribbean and were both unloading at the time. The *Michael David* had a big cargo of lard aboard. The yellow lard came in square five-gallon tins, with plastic tops. Perhaps three hundred of these containers were already stacked on the dock and more still lay on the *Michael David's* deck. Her crew unloaded them from the hold with a sling and swung them ashore on wooden pallets using the foresail boom.

We watched as Buster powered into the harbor at full speed. We could see him standing at the wheel, holding it with one hand and looking as casual as ever. Dad and I hid behind the tins of lard, as he didn't particularly want Buster to know he was spying on him. Suddenly, I sensed my father tense as the *Le Voyageur* continued down the channel at full speed. Being a heavy vessel, he knew she would take a long time to stop.

He began to growl under his breath, "Slow down, Buster, slow down."

The *Le Voyageur* closed the distance to the dock very quickly and we watched as Jongue raced aft to the wheel, glancing nervously towards the docks, which were closing in at an alarming rate. Buster, however, seemed oblivious to the impending danger. His chest was all puffed out, his chin high, resembling a rooster.

Eventually, it dawned on Captain Buster Grant that he was in trouble. Jongue attempted to take the wheel, but now in a state of shock, Buster's hands were locked to the helm like steel vices as *Le Voyageur* plowed spiritedly on, making a bullseye for the *Michael David*.

The trader's crew ceased what they were doing when they saw the big schooner bearing down on them. Like so many varmints abandoning a sinking ship, they quickly leapt ashore.

"Stop, Buster, for God's sake, stop!" yelled my father, but it was to no avail.

We watched in horror as the *Le Voyageur's* long bowsprit struck the *Michael David's* wooden bulwarks at a good ten knots, stoving them in and rolling her over a good thirty-five degrees. Dozens of the lard tins on her deck flew into the air, landing on the dock where they burst open. The heavy two-inch steel wire bobstay under the schooner's bowsprit came up like a giant hacksaw blade, cutting into the hull of the wooden trader. Buster's body loosened up enough for him to faint on the deck and Jongue rang the engine room telegraphs to stop.

As the last lard container rolled to a stop on the wharf, I dared to sneak a look at my father, expecting to find him absolutely furious. Instead, I found him covered from head to foot in half melted slimy lard. I couldn't help but laugh for a moment. He climbed over the *Michael David* onto the *Le Voyageur* by way of her bowsprit, which was still embedded in the trading schooner's pilot house. Taking control, he backed the schooner away and brought her alongside the wharf astern of the *Michael David*.

By the time we got the schooner settled at the dock, Buster had revived. He finally summoned up the courage to approach my father, who was busy toweling himself off by the boarding ladder. Poor Buster looked very shaky as he apologized to my father, who wasn't having any of it.

"Buster, I've been around too long in this game, so don't give me that bull. You just made a bollocks of it and that's that." he said.

When Buster muttered dejectedly about going to pack his bags, my father said something that surprised everyone within earshot.

"Oh, no you don't. You'll get this schooner fueled up and take her back to Marigot, while I stay and sort out this mess here. Only, this time you'll remember what I taught you." he said.

Buster looked a little stupefied, but he picked his sorry self up and went back to work.

This time he took the schooner away from the dock and down to Marigot without a single strut down the deck. He had learned a tough lesson and for the rest of his tenure was a most cautious captain.

The seamen of the island trading schooners, however, apprised *Le Voyageur* with great suspicion thereafter, and would scamper ashore whenever she came into the harbor.

My mother deducted $500 from Buster's wages over the ensuing months to help cover the damage to the *Michael David*.

Harbinger at West End dock where the BVI marine patrol crashed their boat into the dock and face planted the instructor into the concrete dock.

SALVAGE

Who could have known that a Nova Scotian would one day command a fine classic in the southern latitudes? It was one of those beautiful days in Sir Francis Drake Channel. Our 117-foot teak ketch, Harbinger, was sailing well as we made our way to our destination at the Treasure Point anchorage. It was a popular anchorage, with a cave and underwater entrance to the sea. We would often take our charter guests snorkeling in this cave to where the light penetrated with the sun's rays. Outside the cave, you could find various kinds of tropical fish like parrotfish, blowfish, and dozens of other species.

We lowered our sails and after squaring them away we launched the 16-foot rubber Zodiac launch. That evening, our cook served an excellent lobster dinner and after a few drinks our guests went to bed.

Next morning, at about six, I took Matt our deckhand and we made our way to the cave so that he would know where to take our guests snorkeling. The bay was empty as Matt and I motored around Treasure Point, but it was then that we spotted the almost sunk twin outboard speedboat about 300 yards out and we went over to have a look. She was about 25 to 35 feet long, with three big outboards in the range of 200 hp each. A drug boat for sure.

So, we sped back to the Harbinger and picked up our gasoline powered emergency pump. Going back to the swamped speedboat we towed her back to the Harbinger and tied her up alongside.

After pumping her out, we took some gear off. There were two very large and expensive looking fishing rods and strangely in a box under the main thwart there were at least two dozen jars of olives. We thought this was odd to say the least.

There was something fishy going on here. So, getting on the marine VHF radio, I contacted the Tortola marine patrol. They showed up in about twenty minutes, and after discussing the circumstances under which we salvaged this craft, the police towed her away towards the beach. We did note that on the way to the beach, as they towed the small boat, they completely swamped it.

And so, we thought that was the end of that. Little did we know.

On our next charter cruise sailing down Sir Francis Drake Channel, we saw that Commander Blunt, who was the English Commander training the Tortola Marine Police had renovated our salvaged boat and was using it as a patrol boat.

I was not particularly thrilled about this. My crew and I had pumped it out, saved it, and now he was using it as his patrol boat. So, like any fair-minded individual I went to court and pleaded for some payment for my trouble. Blunt was forbidden to use it pending judgment. Needless to say, he was not amused.

One day we had the Harbinger tied up to the end of the T at the marina at West End Tortola taking on water and fuel and who did we see coming towards us. You guessed it. Blunt and his new 40-foot patrol boat and it looked as though he was coming alongside Harbinger. Sarah became quite uneasy about this and disappeared into the deck house. But then he turned to go on the inside of the concrete dock where we were moored.

I was in the deck house with Sarah but at the last moment I decided to be a good chap and go to help him with his patrol boat that was being driven by one of the local Tortola constables from the flying bridge. As he turned to come in on the other side of the concrete dock Blunt took some rope for the bowline and went to the bow pulpit and made to throw it on the dock where I was standing. The patrol boat seemed to be going a bit too fast as it came into the slot. At the very last moment even as it was almost touching the dock the driver threw it into full astern.

Unfortunately, this was enough to launch Blunt over the bow pulpit where he face-planted on the concrete dock at my feet. His lip was bleeding and he looked rather upset. I grabbed him by the shoulder, pulled him on the dock, and asked him if he was alright. After some swearing and glaring. he declared himself to be alright.

Sometimes you just can't win.

Stingray, "Don't step on me!"

The Stingray

The Bahamian islands stretch more than twelve-hundred miles from the latitude of northern Florida to the Dominican Republic in the south. Thousands of low sandy islands and small cays lay on a vast shallow underwater plateau, interspersed with miles of coral reef. Great expanses of turtle grass and sandbanks stretch for miles before dropping into the abyssal Atlantic. The whole area is a fisherman's paradise.

Our ketch, the *High Barbaree*, was built with shallow water cruising in mind, and with her centerboard up she drew only six feet. This gave us access to the scores of small coves and out of the way locations unreachable by other sailing yachts of our size. We carried out many charter cruises in The Bahamas over the years and our guests thrilled at the fantastic fishing and unspoiled anchorages. Even in the mid-eighties the marine life was still abundant, and from time to time, I indulged my life-long love of snorkeling the reef.

The waters of this sprawling archipelago were unfailingly clear, and visibility could be as much as a hundred feet. Many different species of coral grew side-by-side on the reef, creating an amazing and often macabre undersea landscape. Huge coral heads, some the size of a car rose from the sandy bottom and schools of brightly colored fish hugged these massifs for security. Quite often the large holes at the bases of these living polyp colonies were home to large grouper. Antler and staghorn corals branched out in the shallower areas, providing shelter for copper sweepers and glass-eyed snappers. Areas of clumpy bottom, where sand and low corals met, held sea fans and sponges of a dozen different sizes and shapes. Red, schoolmaster, and yellowtail snappers patrolled here, while the tasty mutton and lane snappers rooted in adjacent sandy areas. Grunts and porgies wandered over the sand as well, taking small grubs and shrimp.

We often went bugging on the banks for Panulirus argus, the spiny lobster, called bugs because of their long feelers. We would look for sandy spots in the great expanses of turtle grass because quite often there would be lobsters hiding under the overhanging ledges. Although the bugs themselves were not always visible from the surface, their long undulating feelers were a sure giveaway. We found that the easiest way to catch them was to use a snare, which was simply a stick with a wire loop at the end. We would dive down a few feet to where the lobsters were hiding, slide the wire loop over one of the long feelers and pull it tight. The bug would flip around a bit as it was pulled from its hiding place, but we usually wore a glove on one hand to grab them with.

We carried spear guns on the yacht of the type made famous by the Arbalete Company of France. Their longstanding design consisted of a sturdy aluminum tube connected to a pistol grip handle at one end and a special fitting at the other end which held a spear guide with screw sockets for the rubber slings. The steel spear slid in from the front to lock within the pistol grip. The gun was loaded by pulling rubber slings with stainless steel yokes back to hook into notches in the spear.

We used these undersea hunting rifles to take hogfish, grouper, and snapper for the pot. For the most part we would free dive in waters not deeper than thirty feet.

We saw sharks from time to time, occasionally large ones, but they usually swam off after giving us only the most cursory of looks. I suspect that there was so much food available, that they just weren't hungry, but in most cases, humans just weren't on their normal menu.

The barracudas seemed to be everywhere. I can't remember one occasion when we went spear fishing that we didn't spot a roaming 'cuda. And if there wasn't one in the immediate vicinity when we first entered the water, one would inevitably show up after only a few minutes. They were disconcerting at times, especially those that grew to six feet, and they had a habit of suddenly appearing behind one's back. Hanging almost motionless in the water with the sun rippling off their backs and silver sides, they would work their jaws slowly as if anticipating their next bite. I've been told that this is how they pass oxygen over their gills. They are predators, however, and I once had a very large fellow come in at speed to take a small hogfish off my spear.

Although I've never heard of a deliberate attack by a barracuda, there was the rare accident. These fish, during their natural feeding habits would strike with incredible speed at shiny prey, and the lures we used to catch them were not unlike the shiny band of a wristwatch or bangle. We always advised our guests to remove any glittering jewelry before swimming or snorkeling, just in case a 'cuda mistook it for its dinner.

One of our favorite seafoods was conch, those huge mollusks used to make the famous Bahamian conch chowder. These tasty shellfish could be found in great profusion on the turtle grass beds as well as on the vast open sandbanks. Here, in these shallow areas, the southern stingray was a frequent visitor, skimming the bottom in search of food.

I credited myself with being a careful diver and always advised guests not to disturb any undersea life that could be dangerous. Over many years of snorkeling and diving, I only had one accident and it was due entirely to my own carelessness.

Having just ended a two-week charter in Nassau, my crew and I were looking forward to some relaxation. We decided to anchor off Frazer's Hog Cay in the Berry Islands for few days of spear fishing and bottom jigging. Towards mid-afternoon, I managed to talk the others into a conch chowder, and they agreed as long as I would come up with the conch. This large mollusk was so plentiful in those years that you could wade along in ankle deep water near the shore and pick them up. So, after telling my crew that I would be back before dark, I left in the thirteen-foot ship's dinghy.

Locating a bank of turtle grass just around the point from the anchored yacht, I donned mask and fins and went into the water. Pulling the dinghy along behind me as I swam, I soon began to find the odd shell. After a while, the water got too shallow to swim in, and because there seemed to be even more conchs in the shallower water, I removed my mask and fins and proceeded along by foot. After tilting the outboard motor up, I put the bowline over my shoulder and continued to pull the boat astern of me.

Evening was coming, but I could still see the big shells as they appeared on the bottom and, after another fifteen minutes, I had collected about two dozen. Quite suddenly, the wind began to pipe up and a short chop came up. It was still too shallow to use the outboard and so I continued to pull the boat towards the anchorage.

I had been told a long time ago by local fishermen to shuffle my feet along the bottom when wading in the shallows, to scare up any stingrays that might be around. I was doing just that, I thought, but suddenly my foot came down on something live. It took me only a second to realize that I had stepped on something other than the bottom. First, I felt the rough surface of the skin wiggling under my foot, and a split second later I felt a sharp pain in my calf. A stingray had barbed me. Quickly jumping into the dinghy, I looked down in horror. There was two inches of grey stingray barb sticking out of my lower calf. Surprisingly, there was only a tiny trickle of blood, but I could see the traces of milky white toxin on the thing, and even though it had not yet taken effect I knew I was in trouble.

Taking a pair of pliers from the box I pulled the barb out, which was buried an inch deep. Darkness was falling and I was still half a mile from the anchorage. My crew had no way of knowing I was in trouble. Stupidly, I had broken my own rule of always having a redundancy. Now I would pay for it.

Getting back into the water wasn't my first choice, but I had to do it so I could pull the dinghy back into deeper water, and thus be able to use the outboard. I hoped I wouldn't step on yet another stingray, and luckily, I didn't. Finally, just as the pain in my leg really began to hurt, I was able to push the boat into deeper water and start the outboard. The throbbing pain was excruciating by the time I came alongside the *High Barbaree*. We quickly heaved up the anchor and went into the marina, where I was able to seek the help of a doctor.

He gave me a tetanus shot, but by the next day my lower leg had swollen up to the size of a tree trunk. I suffered a tremendous infection, which took more than a month to fully dissipate, but eventually my leg returned to normal.

I'll be the first to admit that the whole thing was my own fault. The ray probably wasn't a very big fellow, but certainly the sting of this ray was enough to cause me a lot of pain and misery. The moral of this story is to always watch where you put your feet.

ROACHES IN PARADISE

The Barton's were a party of six who had flown in from California for a week-long cruise of the Virgin Islands. The *High Barbaree* was fueled and provisioned, and we were ready to go. I sent the two deckhands up to the parking lot behind the marina to meet our guests, and after about twenty minutes, they appeared at the head of the dock pushing a trolley load of suitcases. I was standing by to greet them at the gangway. A tall, broad-shouldered gentleman was first at the rail. He seemed to be about fortyish, sporting a gold Rolex and Gucci shoes.

"Mr. Barton, welcome aboard the *High Barbaree*." I said offering my hand.

"You the skipper?" he asked brusquely while stepping onto the deck. He ignored my proffered hand.

"Yes," I replied smiling, turning to shake hands with his wife and the other two couples.

The crew carried their fifteen pieces of luggage over the rail and disappeared below, while I ushered our passengers down the companionway to the deck salon. Mrs. Barton looked around as if puzzled by something. It wasn't long before I got the first inkling that something was wrong. The giant cruise liner Norwegian Prince was berthed across the bay alongside the tourist wharf, and I noticed Mrs. Barton looking over towards her.

"I thought we were going on that." she said sounding annoyed.

"No Jeannie, I told you we were going on a sailing yacht." he replied in an exasperated tone.

She gave him a sneer and turned to me.

"It's boiling in here. Don't you have the air conditioning on?" she asked me. "And where's the casino? Don't you have a casino aboard?"

I looked at her to see if she was serious. She was.

"There's no casino, and no air conditioning either." I replied. "But, we have lots of hatches and portholes and the ocean breeze keeps us cool." I explained helpfully.

Mrs. Barton seemed rather piqued at this information and affected a swoon to the settee, fanning herself with her hand, even though there was a nice cool breeze coming through the overhead hatch.

The stewardess showed the other guests to their cabins and explained about the heads, but it wasn't long before the first complaints began to come.

"The cabins are too small...," "The cabins are way too hot...," or "The beds are too narrow..."

Mrs. Barton continued to gaze at the cruise liner. Then she turned to her husband.

"Charlie baby, I wanna go on that one." she whined, pointing at the Norwegian Prince, "It's got air conditioning, a casino aboard, and a swimming pool. You know how I hate to swim in the ocean."

"But honey, we've already paid half the charter fee for this boat." he pointed out.

"Honey," she sat there pouting.

Mr. Barton and I sat down at the navigation table on the other side of the saloon to sort out the paperwork and collect the balance of the charter fee, which was due upon boarding. Before I got around to it, Charlie pulled out a small tourist map of the West Indies and laid it on the table.

"Before I hand over any more bucks, skipper, I'd like to make sure you can take us where we wanna' go." he said.

"Fine. Let's have a look." I replied, trying to keep an open mind. But as soon as I looked at his map, I knew there was going to be trouble. There were masses of red dots lined all the way from Puerto Rico to Venezuela. Our week-long cruise was scheduled for the Virgin Islands. However, I gave him my compete attention.

"First, we wanna see the Virgin Islands, then we wanna go visit Barbosa." he began.

I assumed he was talking about Barbados, but I said nothing.

"Then," he continued, "We wanna take a look at Trinidad and Venezuela. Whatever time we have left after that, we can use in Puerto Rico. My little wife wants to do some gambling there."

I mulled this over for a second, trying to figure out how to explain. Obviously, the man had no idea about the distances that a 78-foot sailboat could cover in a week. I turned to him again, trying hard to smile.

"Mr. Barton, as much as I'd like to take you to all these places, it's just not possible."

"What, you mean you won't take us to Barbosa?" he asked scowling.

"It's not that I won't, sir," I offered. "It's just not physically possible to move this type of yacht around to all these places in the short period you have booked. A big cruise liner may be able to do it, but not a sailboat."

He contemplated what I said for a moment.

"Right then, I want my money back." he demanded sounding a bit belligerent.

"But you haven't even paid me the balance yet." I said sensing that trouble was seriously on its way.

"I already paid you two thousand dollars when I booked this goddamn holiday." he said his voice rising.

"You paid the deposit only, Mr. Barton, and I've already spent most of it. We take half the cost of the charter so we can fuel up the boat, buy all the groceries for the week, and pay the crew. We do all this before you arrive."

That did it for Mr. Barton. He turned angrily to his wife.

"Come on honey, we're getting off this goddamn barge." he barked and then he ordered my crew to get their luggage off.

My venerable Philip Rhodes ketch, although not new, was certainly not a barge. I was offended.

As I watched the Barton party disappear up the dock towards the marina office, I pondered the fact that in all the time I have operated a charter boat, I have never had a party walk away like this. What I didn't know then was that I hadn't seen the last of our Mr. Barton.

I immediately went up to the charter agent who had booked the charter and asked for her opinion. She advised me to keep the yacht at the dock with a full crew aboard, ready to carry out our side of the contract if Mr. Barton decided to return. A highly unlikely scenario, I thought.

At about three in the afternoon on our second day of standby, Mr. Barton came strolling down the dock with a shoe box under his arm. I met him at the rail.

"Can I come aboard?" he asked cordially.

"Certainly," I replied. "Your charter is ready to go anytime you want."

"I told you we ain't going anywhere on this thing. I want my money back." he responded gruffly. "Are you going to give it to me?"

"I've already explained the situation to you sir." I replied.

"Right," he says taking the shoe box from under his arm, "If you don't give me my money back, I'm going straight to the charter office to show them this."

He opened the shoe box just enough so I could take a quick peep. I could hardly believe what this guy was thinking of. Inside the box there were about six of the giant palmetto cockroaches that are common in the islands. I couldn't help but chuckle as I shook my head in wonder.

"And just what are you going to say when you go the charter office?" I asked him, my patience starting to wane.

"I'm going to tell them that I found these on your boat, behind the toilet." he told me with a straight face.

"Oh, that's original. Well then, you go right ahead." I replied, feeling really teed off with this nut. "Give it your best shot."

He replaced the lid, gave me a furious look, and walked briskly up the dock. The following morning, I received a call from the charter office. The fellow had indeed shown the shoe box of cockroaches to our agent, saying that he had found them aboard the *High Barbaree*, and that was the reason he didn't want to make the cruise. They laughed him out the door, for they knew our boat well. I thought that would be the last of it, but it was not to be so.

On the evening of the fifth day of the ill-fated charter, we were still at the marina dock following the advice of our agent, ready to fulfil our contract commitment, if required. Three oddly dressed folks came walking down the dock to where we were tied up. There were two men and a woman. They certainly looked as though they were from the shadier side of town. They handed me an envelope.

"Captain,

Seeing as how I have already paid you for our cruise you can take these friends out for a week. You can also supply them with their drinking requirements.

Charlie Barton."

The taller of the two men waited for me to finish reading the note.

"So, when can we get this thing going?" he asked.

"We aren't going anywhere." I replied. "Barton only paid the deposit."

"OK, looks like I'm gonna have to get tough with you. He told me moving to put his foot on the rail."

I've always been known as an easy-going chap, but clearly this had gotten out of hand.

"Listen mister, if you set foot on my deck, I'm going to just set you back on the dock." I stepped to the rail and my six-foot-four frame left no doubt that I would do what I said.

The mate took off to get the marina police officer and they showed up a moment later.

"Having a little trouble skipper?" the officer asked.

"Yes sir."

"We'll just sort this out then." he said. "OK bud, we'll just take a little walk, taking my wanna-be passenger by the elbow and ushering him down the dock. Clearly, they had made their acquaintance before.

Ah, the joys of the yacht charter business.

I am aboard Bluenose II, second from right.

I⸳LAND ⸳QUALL

Those of us who sail the Caribbean long enough eventually taste the wrath of a real West Indian squall. Over the years charter skipper colleagues of mine have recounted tales of particularly nasty squalls with winds to 55 or more knots. What follows is my recollection of a proper stinker.

In 1967 I was a 17-year-old deckhand on the great schooner *Bluenose II*. At 143 feet, she was big and every bit as fast as her namesake. We had just finished a charter in Martinique the day before and were running into the Anegada passage bound for St Thomas. It was a windy dawn to start with, but I'll let my notes tell the tale.

Skodge and the skipper stand with legs spread and hands fastened to the brass guardrail surrounding the helm while the rest of us remain huddled behind the canvas dodger, an unwilling audience to a dismal panorama. None of us has slept; the tortured noises our hull is making below decks along with the violent motion rule out any notions of rest. Some of us are exhilarated but all of us are afraid. I am in total awe of the scene that lies before me.

The sea has built through the night and in the grayness of the morning the great Atlantic swells chase us down. Ghostly thirty-footers rise like mountains off our quarter before breaking in white foaming crests. Like malevolent giants they tower over the ship before rushing down towards us, angry avalanches of ocean. It seems that every wave will certainly come aboard and swallow us, but our schooner bravely lifts her hip and the sea rolls beneath the keel, lifting us and thrusting us even faster through the water. As we careen madly down the steep slopes, the knot meter jumps. I watch mesmerized as it climbs to 12, 13, and 14 knots before the schooner shudders as she reaches the bottoms of the troughs and slows to the more credible 10-11 knots.

The sea and wind leave us in no doubt that we are within Anegada's embrace now. On the crests, the *Bluenose II* stands upright, and her fourteen thousand square feet of canvas catches the full brunt of the wind. She reaps her power then, shaking and shuddering, and throwing a white bow wave 100 feet to leeward.

The squall hits suddenly, coming out of the dawn horizon like a dark ghost. The wind increases until the anemometer holds at about 40 knots. We look to the skipper to see if he will order us to strike topsails but there is a grim determination in his face.

"OK, let's run her off now." he shouts to the helmsman over the whine of the wind.

But he is interrupted by a loud crack and the schooner trembles and shakes as if she has been struck. The fisherman topsail peak halyard has parted, and the peak of the sail is trailing out to leeward, flogging like crazy. The whipping sail cracks and snaps so loudly that it is clearly audible above the wind, and then as we look on in disbelief the sheet rips the clew out adding more loose canvas to the fray. The bosun runs forward to the foremast pin rail, throwing off the halyard but nothing happens; the throat block has shattered under the strain and the sail is jammed aloft. Small bits of wood from the cheeks fly away to leeward as the block disintegrates completely leaving only the metal frame and sheave with the jammed halyard inside. A stronger gust hits the schooner, and she trembles as if shaken by a giant hand.

"You need to get that sail off her before it shakes the rig to pieces." the skipper shouts.

There is a certain breed of seaman worth his weight in gold and the bosun is one. But he will need help.

"I'll go with you." a voice calls, but as I look around to see which fool has spoken, I realize that it is I.

"Alright, just you hold on boyo, it's going to be a rough one up there.

The bosun leads and I follow him up the foremast starboard ratlines. The shrouds are taught as guitar strings. The heavy wire cables vibrate with the strain, and I feel sure that they will part at any moment. Halfway up, I pause momentarily as the wind tries to pluck me from the rig and I find myself using all my strength to hold on. The bosun reaches the crosstrees and pulling his Dexter seaman's knife he positions himself to make the cut, but he cannot lean out far enough; he needs my help. He looks down at me, to see if I will make it to the top. My guts are tight, and the wind whips my hair as if to scalp me but suddenly the fear passes, and I know that I can do it. I am a seaman, and this is my work, the uneasiness disappears to be replaced with an almost reckless exhilaration and I smile slightly as I climb the last forty feet to the crosstrees. Perhaps I am going mad; who would smile at this time? It's wild and windy 100 feet above the deck and as the schooner rolls, so her spars trace wide arcs across the dark sky. The bosun's a strong man and hard as nails but the huge wooden foremast is shaking like a leaf in the wind and we both struggle to save ourselves from being flung off. The view is unbelievable. The schooner's hull seems like a tiny splinter of wood in the huge seas. Every few moments her lovely form disappears completely as a wave hits and flying spray covers her. It's distressing when we see only her spars rising out of the sea of angry spray.

"Hold me as I cut." He yells brandishing his knife in his right hand. His left is locked to the crosstrees with a vice like grip

Gripping the crosstrees with my legs I grasp the bosun around the waist with my left arm while holding the throat halyard with my right. It is all I can do to hold him, but he leans out quickly with the knife and places the sharp blade to the bar-tight halyard. It needs only two or three slices before the line explodes with a bang and suddenly the shaking stops. The already tattered fisherman topsail flies away to leeward and is still airborne when it disappears from view some three hundred yards away. The mast is saved and the schooner sails on. Back on the deck I can hardly believe what I have done.

"Hell of a job boys." the skipper tells us, and I feel satisfied with our accomplishment, but his next sentence shocks us.

"Set the quine staysail." Captain Coggins orders.

We look at him as if he is mad; perhaps he is. The wind is on the quarter at 35 knots, and the *Bluenose II* surges ahead.

The quine staysail is a small jib shaped sail that is set between the topmasts. It's much smaller than the fisherman topsail but when the *Bluenose II* is in the deep troughs between the waves and hidden from the main force of the wind this sail will steady her. It will be the highest one, like a kite flying from the main topmast. Setting it from the deck we trim it up for the slant and at 14 knots we run on towards St. Thomas."

This was the one that bit the owner's New rubber Zodiac boat!

OF BARRACUDAS AND MEN

The *Harbinger* was a classic sailing vessel that my wife and I had the privilege of commanding from mid-1994 to the middle of 1996. She was the epitome of the classic sailing yacht, with enough brass and varnish to keep you going full-time. From her long bowsprit to graceful counter stern, her long sheer line was perfect, and her 120-foot. tall main mast seemed to pierce the sky. At 117-feet long with a tonnage of 105, she was a big heavy ketch-rigged yacht.

Built for a Scottish Duke by Stowe Brothers in Shoreham, England, she was constructed totally of teak and commissioned in 1913. The fact that she lived so long is a testament to her builders. She has outlasted them all.

With a crew of seven, we sailed the *Harbinger* to a shipyard and spent 8 months rebuilding her. After major work on her hull the painters sprayed her topsides white, and they glistened in the tropical sun. Skilled tradesmen worked on rigging and sails and repaired or replaced any faulty equipment. Finally, after a mechanical rebuild we took her out for sea trials.

While we were there, the owners decided to replace the aging inflatable Avon speedboat. On a yacht, the dinghy or tender is an important and special piece of equipment. It carries passengers and crew back and forth to the shore. It goes grocery shopping and brings laundry aboard. During leisure time, it takes guests water-skiing or fishing, and ferries them ashore for drinks or dinner in the evening.

Although the old Avon was a good make, our poor thing was just worn out. It lost air all the time and despite continuous patching there was no stopping the bow compartments from deflating. Our deckhands were forever pumping it up but within hours it would deflate again.

With the owner's blessing I selected a brand-new 17-foot Caribe, a rigid bottom inflatable, with a sixty-horsepower outboard motor. It was a real treat to ride in this splendid new speedboat, all white and shiny, with the steering console amidships. The owner of the yacht loved it. It was his personal "toy," and he would speed around for hours in it, going nowhere in particular.

In late 1995, we took the owners and their friends on a cruise around the British Virgin Islands, stopping one day at the picturesque Bitter End anchorage on the island of Virgin Gorda. Hans, one of the owner's friends, was keen on fishing, so I organized an expedition for him.

Early the next morning, we took off in the inflatable towards the reef surrounding the north end of the island to see what we could catch. The sun was rising into a clear blue sky and the weather was gorgeous. It took us only fifteen minutes running at full speed to reach the outside of the reef and then I slowed down. We could see the sandy bottom through the crystal-clear water as it joined the edge of the coral, while further out it sloped gently into the deep. Small fish near the surface darted away as we cruised along and deeper down there was the occasional larger one swimming nearer the bottom. I had a good feeling as I set the rod up for Hans and we began trolling along the edge.

Hans was the impatient type. After only a few minutes he began to give me advice on how to catch fish.

"Zis is crazy, you go too fast."

I slowed the boat down.

"Capitan, now you go too slow, ve vill never catch ze fisch."

I sped up again.

"Capitan, you should know you must use zee lure wiz zee green spots in zee Caribbean, not zee one vith zee red stripe."

Hans had never been to the Caribbean before, but I changed "zee lure" anyway, and that made him happy.

"Capitan, ve must go over zere, zat is vhere zee fisch are."

I steered the boat over there.

After about half an hour of steady instructions from Hans, he got a big strike, bending his rod right over and peeling off yards of line.

"I get zee fisch, I get zee fisch." he shouted triumphantly.

"Great," I replied. "Just reel him in nice and slow. That's it, don't rush, just keep him coming nice and steady."

"Okay, okay," Hans didn't like to be told too much about how to catch "fisch" in the Caribbean. After all, he was the expert now.

As I gave Hans unwanted advice and helped him with the drag, he slowly reeled the fish in. It was heavy and pulled line back out every moment or so. After twenty minutes, we could see a long silvery shape down in the azure depths.

"Look, look, capitan, zee fisch, I can see zee fisch."

As I looked down I recognized the fish. It was a very large barracuda, perhaps five feet long.

"Good going, Hans." I said. "You've caught yourself a big barracuda."

"Vot did you say? A barracuda? It is very dangerous, no?"

Hans's voice had lost its authoritative tone now and he sounded a little concerned.

"No Hans, he's not dangerous, just as long as you keep your fingers out of his mouth." I pointed out, smiling slightly to myself.

Hans continued reeling and I steered the boat until the barracuda was just below the surface. It was a large specimen, so I grabbed the gaff, a long aluminum pole with a nasty hook on the end used for lifting larger fish aboard.

"Just bring him up a little more, and I'll gaff him." I said.

Hans wiped his brow with the back of his hand and cranked a few more turns on the reel. Suddenly, Mr. Barracuda disappeared under the boat and a moment later we heard a loud hissing sound. Glancing over the side of the inflatable, there was a fizz of bubbles coming up from under the boat.

Would you believe it! The damned barracuda had taken a bite at the rubber pontoon and had successfully drawn air, which was now rapidly escaping. Hans looked over at me with a confused expression on his face.

"Vot happens, capitan? Look, zere are many bubbles coming?"

I certainly didn't need Hans to tell me that bubbles were coming, that was pretty clear. I was more concerned about whether we were going to drive or swim home. The air was escaping at a surprising rate and the port side of the Caribe was already deflating.

I quickly opened the little stowage compartment under the seat and pulling out the air pump, I plugged the hose into the air intake port.

"Hans, you pump this as fast as you can while I try and drive us home." I said.

"What about my fisch?"

"I wouldn't worry about the fisch." I said, "You just concentrate on putting air back into this boat before we have to swim for it."

I took his rod and stuck it in the holder on the console and a worried looking Hans began working the pump handle as fast as he could. We headed back to the *Harbinger*, still anchored off the Bitter End yacht club. As we limped along in a rather lopsided fashion, Hans continued to work the hand pump like a demon. He kept glancing over his shoulder to see how far we still had to go. I couldn't go very fast because one side of the boat was dragging in the water. At some point, I noted that we were going to make it all right.

"Keep pumping man," I said. Hans had worked up quite a sweat by then, but he redoubled his efforts. I confess that I was having a little fun with him to get even for all the bossing around he had given me back out at the reef.

We came alongside to find the owner and his friends as well as the crew lining the rail curious to see what was wrong with the speedboat. My boss wasn't too happy. He had spotted Hans' frantic pumping from a ways off and now saw the bubbles. I had somehow managed to put a hole in his new speedboat and I could see that he was thinking I had done something wrong. I tried to explain.

"You just won't believe how this happened." I said, realizing immediately that it probably wasn't a particularly smart way to begin my report.

I continued, "Hans caught a huge barracuda, and, well it came right up under the boat and bit a hole in it."

I realized as soon as I had finished that I sounded ridiculous, and as I looked at the owner, I could see that he was thinking the same thing. He turned to Hans and began speaking rapidly in German. Luckily, Hans saved the day. Smiling, he grabbed his fishing rod from the holder where I had stuck it and started to reel in. The rod tip twitched and bent again, and as the last twenty feet came in, a very large limp barracuda appeared at the end, measuring about five feet long. Somehow, it had stayed hooked as we limped home.

Hans pulled his monster up with the gaff and proudly displayed it for all to see, making sure he kept his fingers away from the wicked looking teeth. He glanced at me with an "I told you so" look.

You see capitan, zee lure wiz zee green spots was correct, ya?"

He then began talking in German with the owner, explaining to him the circumstances surrounding our accident. I managed to pick out a couple of words as he spoke. "Capitan Lou" and "barracuda," popped up regularly.

Afterwards, we hoisted the speedboat back on deck to repair it, and locating the hole, we found the guilty object, an inch-long barracuda tooth embedded in the edge of the rubber seam. I presented it to the owner as a souvenir and he was placated. He was even happier later in the day when we put his patched toy back into the water.

It's probably just as well that he was aboard when this little incident took place. I wonder if he would have believed me had I called on the phone to inform him that a huge fish had bitten a hole in his speedboat

Yankee sailing near Baddeck

The Schooners Yankee, Doubloon, and Windbloweth

Sixty-nine years is a long time. But this story spans these years. I was born in Baddeck, Cape Breton in 1951 and spent my first years growing up on the decks of the famous schooners Yankee and Doubloon. My father, Captain Walter Boudreau had survived near fatal tragedies during the war. The wreck on the northern Labrador coast where his 140-foot schooner Nellie J King had foundered on a lee shore in a storm. Later, his ship the barkentine Angelus had been sunk by a German submarine in the Atlantic and of a crew of eleven, only he and one other survived after ten days in a lifeboat.

But my father Walter Boudreau was one of those Nova Scotian's extraordinaire, blessed with courage and a desire to spend his life under sail.

It was at this time that the world-famous schooner *Yankee* became available for sale, and he partnered with Capt. Frank Swift, of Maine, with the burgeoning start to the Maine windjammer business. Young Capt. Walter later determined that he would start his own business in his home province of Nova Scotia. And so, he purchased Swift's shares in the schooner Yankee and brought her to Baddeck in the Bras d'Or Lakes of Cape Breton. There, he started Nova Scotia Windjammer Cruises, this province's first windjammer cruise business. The *Yankee*, *Doubloon*, and *Windbloweth* made up his fleet.

The summers in the Bras d'Or Lakes were beautiful. Abundant coves and picturesque anchorages abounded, and my father Capt. Walter's schooners carried out week-long cruises in these pristine waters. There were beaches and coves where the ship's cooks prepared lobster boils and clam bakes. The saltwater lakes were calm, and the schooners sailed from anchorage to anchorage, often sailing just below Alexander Graham Bell's majestic home on the hill near Baddeck. Occasionally, the wafting sounds of bagpipes could be heard drifting over the hills. These waters were warmer than the outside Atlantic and swimming was possible. My father, the *Yankee's* captain, would take his passengers ashore to a sandy beach where they could relax; a magic time to be sure.

To say that my father was a visionary would be an understatement. He was correct in knowing that people would pay to sail on these schooners and to experience adventure only as life under sail can provide. There were also trips to the French islands of St. Pierre and Miquelon, and as my mother told me many years later, some of those passengers visiting the French Islands had a suspicious resemblance to wooden barrels. Who knows? Perhaps some of that great sailor's elixir made its way back to Nova Scotia. Needless to say, the evidence would not have lasted long. To say that I remember any of this would be a stretch, but the tales told to me over the years and the photos bring my childhood existence on these schooners to life.

The Windjammer Fleet

Nova Scotia Windjammer Cruises was successful, and many passengers enjoyed the adventure of life under sail in the waters of Nova Scotia's Bras d'Or. But Walter Boudreau had a desire to spend his life under sail full-time and the northern winters prevented enjoyment of those warm summer cruises. Shortly thereafter, as the business developed, more and more passengers came to sail on his schooners.

The epiphany came when my father decided to make a winter trip to the West Indies aboard the *Doubloon* and carry some passengers there, returning for the summer to Cape Breton. It was during this voyage that I almost perished when the surf boat on Saba Rock capsized in the waves. The boat men saved my mother and I, my first taste of respect for the ocean wave.

It was upon this final return that we found the *Yankee* scuttled near Baddeck, a mystery still unsolved. And unbeknownst to mom and me, another of life's voyages had begun.

Today the waters of Nova Scotia hide the wreck of the schooner *Yankee*. Although this schooner was extremely famous in her heyday; it is a little-known fact that her hull lies in a secluded cove in the Bras d'Or Lakes of Cape Breton. Her hull is for the most part intact although she has been picked clean of artifacts over the decades. It is even a less-

Nova Scotia Windjammer cruises brochures

er-known fact that the gimballed wardroom table had lead ingots dove up from the *HMS Bounty* at Pitcairn's Island.

History of the famed schooner *Yankee*

The schooner *Yankee* was born *Lood Schooner 4* in Holland as a Dutch pilot schooner. These vessels were designed to go out in all weather, bringing bigger ships and pilots to Dutch ports. They needed to be robust and weatherly and certainly, the schooner *Yankee* was that. She was very heavily built with a sea kindly hull shape and high bulwarks all around. Her moderate gaff rig was easily handled and reefed and the *Yankee* no doubt weathered many North Sea storms before finding a new home in Gloucester, Massachusetts.

Capt. Irving Johnson, a great seaman, was one owner of the *Yankee* before my father. In his early days he was lucky enough to have experienced some of the last great days of sailing on big square riggers rounding Cape Horn. He later had this idea that people would pay to experience a more moderate version of this kind of adventure under sail. He

Yankee spreads her wings in a light breeze.

was right. However, he needed a real seagoing vessel, small enough for his purposes and yet big enough to accommodate some paying amateur crew. When he bought the schooner *Yankee* in 1933, he knew he had found the right vessel. Under his able command Captain Irving Johnson sailed the schooner *Yankee* around the world three times. His first voyage was recounted in the book *Westward Bound in the Schooner Yankee* in 1936.

His crews experienced real-life adventure that regular folk could only imagine. There were coral atolls and reefs, palmed-lined beaches, remote tribes in New Guinea, and a thousand other extraordinary experiences. All this while sailing a fine schooner across the oceans of the world with the trade winds at her back.

After the Second World War, the Boudreau family bought and operated the *Yankee* along with their other two schooners as the Windjammer Cruise company in the Bras d'Or Lakes in Cape Breton, Canada. After the short summers, they would voyage south to cruise the winters in the warm waters of the Caribbean. The Boudreau family went on to pioneer the sailing business in the West Indies owning some sixteen vessels over the years.

After the short summers, they would voyage south to cruise the winters in the warm waters of the Caribbean. Sadly, when the *Yankee* was left moored one winter, she sank under mysterious circumstances.

The schooner *Yankee* inspired hundreds, if not thousands, to emulate her high seas adventures. Tall ship training and adventure sailing has grown over the years and there are now many vessels in the trade. But it all began with the schooner *Yankee* and now, my dream is that hopefully she will sail again one day, a ghost from the past that will spread her white wings to grace the oceans once more.

Schooner Doubloon
One fleet of the Nova Scotia Windjammer Cruises.

MAMA D'LEAU

In the eighties we sailed the High Barbaree on her charter cruises in the West Indies and when we were not busy, we moored her in the protective double lagoons of beautiful Marigot Bay, St. Lucia. Perhaps the best natural harbor in the Windward Islands; Marigot has a secret inner lagoon that is not visible from the sea.

This fascinating island was fought over for almost twenty-five years by the British and French and changed hands no less than fourteen times. Some of the islanders speak English but for the most part they speak the local patios, a form of much broken French.

Legend has it that a part of the British fleet under Admiral Sir Samuel Barrington hid his ships in Marigot Bay allowing the French to sail by to leeward. He subsequently was able to sail out and defeat them having the windward position.

Before the arrival of cheap Japanese outboard motors, the local fishermen went to sea in traditional Gomier canoes, cranky craft with flour bag sails. First built by some unknown Carib or Arawak Indian ages ago. These dugout canoes had changed little from the original form, a design passed down from generation to generation. The present-day fishermen and seafarers of these islands were for the most part descendants of the African slaves brought to the Caribbean many years ago. Their culture was rich in folk superstition, and many a tale was told to me over the years,

There were many tales told of unusual happenings both above and below the surface of the Caribbean. One in particular intrigued me. It was the legend of the "Mama D'Leau, literally translated "Water Mama" or in English lexicon, mermaid.

According to the local fishermen these lovely creatures were found offshore, where the lee of the island meets the deep blue of the Caribbean. Half woman and half fish, they were not held to be inherently dangerous, but it was believed that men were unable to resist their call. I was told that many fishermen over the years had succumbed and never returned to port. Apparently, these sirens were able to lure sailors far out to sea where they would then entice them beneath the surface. If a fishing canoe went missing, then a Mama D'Leau was responsible. The recovery of an empty canoe at sea was an indication that this mysterious female creature had been in the vicinity.

One winter, we concluded a two-week charter of the Grenadines on the *High Barbaree* and after disembarking our party in St. Vincent, we set sail for St. Lucia. Although the trade winds were light that day, the big steel ketch sailed well on the starboard tack. However, as the day wore on the breeze pulled to the north and by the time we were under the lee of St. Lucia we found ourselves about ten miles offshore.

I didn't mind, it was a beautiful day and the blue Caribbean to the west of the island was calm as a millpond. Off our bow, flying fish left the surface in their dozens and like tiny silver missiles flew a hundred yards or more before plopping back into the sea. With the vessel close hauled we sailed the long tack north until we were abeam of the port of Castries. After taking a bearing, I felt that we were high enough to windward to fetch our destination of Marigot Bay, and so we came about.

It was then that we spotted the boat. About three miles away and shoreward of us a single occupant paddled a tiny skiff. Making a change of course to pass close to the little boat we slowly closed the distance. As we approached, I looked through the binoculars. It became apparent that something was amiss. The tiny wooden craft was no more than twelve feet long and in a poor state of repair. Her captain appeared to be a fisherman in tattered trousers and denim shirt paddling in a desperate manner using a broken oar.

The odd thing was that he was moving in a southwesterly direction, away from the land towards South America, many hundreds of miles away. What could this fellow be up to, I wondered? I luffed as we came alongside him, and my mate called to the skiff.

"Aye man, what happen wid you nuh?"

There was no answer, but the man redoubled his efforts with the broken oar.

"Hey," I called as he passed our stern, "What are you doing?"

It seemed that the fellow was either mad, or bent on self-destruction, and so reluctantly I gave the order to strike sail and starting the main engine we began to lower away.

By the time I turned the vessel around under power the skiff had made another hundred yards to the west. Bringing the ketch alongside him again we offered a line, but he refused to take it.

"Mama D'Leau ka couya mwe," he shouted over and over in the local St. Lucian patois language.

I resolved that the fellow must not be allowed to drown whatever the reason for his madness, and I had the mate lower the accommodation ladder and put a line on his bow the next time I came alongside. He tried to resist but we took him bodily aboard, leaving his decrepit skiff to tow astern.

Laying a course back towards the port of Castries we turned our attention to the man we had pulled from an almost certain death on the sea. He was well-built, sporting a bushy beard, and closely trimmed hair. But it was his eyes that startled me. They were stark and wild, as if telling of some supernatural experience.

In Patois the mate asked him what he was doing so far out, paddling for Venezuela as fast as he could.

"De Mama D'Leau, she calling me," he managed in broken English.

I turned to the mate.

"What does he mean she's calling him?" I asked, "Who is Mama D'leau anyway?"

"He says that de Mama D'Leau was calling him and he had to go."

The mate's matter of fact tone suggested that this was explanation enough for the fisherman's bizarre actions. We gave him sweet coffee and the cook brought a large piece of the fried tuna we had enjoyed for lunch. He wolfed this down and after some further questioning we managed to piece together his strange tale.

The man had been fishing in Castries harbor when a Mama D'Leau surfaced near his craft. He explained that the creature had so beguiled him that he had been forced to follow as she led him from the relative safety of the bay to the open Caribbean. We asked why he had not tried to resist. He replied that this was impossible; did we not understand the powers of the Mama D'Leau?

MAMA D'LEAU

We took him to the mouth of Castries harbor where the police launch came out. As we handed him over and cast off the skiff, I pondered our recent experience. Initially I felt sorely cheated that I had not seen the mermaid, but then, would I not have succumbed to her irresistible call as well? As we made our way south to Marigot Bay I decided that I would happily settle for second best. I had not seen the mermaid, but certainly I had witnessed the behavior of one man who had.

PERFIDIOUS ALBION

During the years we spent sailing in the West Indies, there were some pretty remarkable occurrences, funny and otherwise. Some were hard to believe, and the following incident certainly falls under that heading.

We have all heard stories of insurance fraud and in the summer of 1974, my brother Pete and I saw a truly brazen example. Our charter schooner *Janeen* usually spent the most dangerous months of the hurricane season anchored in the inner lagoon of Marigot Bay, St. Lucia, which would provide good shelter in the event of a storm.

Mr. and Mrs. Higgins-Smythe were an English couple living on the island at that time. In his early sixties, he was affiliated with Lloyd's insurance in the capacity of a post loss investigator and based on the island. They owned a pretty little red sloop of about thirty feet that they kept moored at the Yacht Haven hotel in Marigot Bay. The Yacht Haven hotel was a small operation owned by our family. In those years there was little summer tourism, and the hotel was closed for the quiet months.

The Higgins-Smythe's would drive down to Marigot on the weekends to take their sloop out for cruises along the coast, anchoring occasionally in a secluded cove for a swim. Their yacht had a good-looking steel hull, giving her a rugged capability superior to her wooden or fiberglass cousins. She had a varnished spruce wooden mast and new white sails. The couple always seemed happy with their little sloop and whenever I spoke to them, they were cheerful and most polite.

One morning, Pete and I were walking past the dock in front of the hotel, when we noticed something odd. Mr. and Mrs. Higgins-Smythe were aboard their sloop and seemed to be stripping it. There was no other way to describe what was taking place. They were hard at work unloading any gear that could be removed and putting it onto the dock. There was a pile of life jackets, linen, mattresses, flares, tools and even a nice-looking marine toilet already sitting there. They even removed the stove and all the crockery and food stocks.

As Pete and I stopped to watch them, they appeared very ill at ease and seemed to be wishing that we would just move on and leave them. I was intrigued.

"Doing a little overhaul are you?" I asked innocently.

Mr. Higgins-Smythe looked at me with an annoyed expression and answered rather abruptly. "Yes, and we'd like to get on with it without interruption, if you don't mind."

Later that day, Pete and I were standing on the veranda of our parents' home, which stood on the southern bluff of Marigot and gave a sweeping unobstructed view of the entire bay. We noticed the little red sloop coming slowly down the channel, heading for the open sea. We could see Mr. Higgins-Smythe standing at the helm, while his wife was busy doing something in the cockpit. Unaware they were being watched, they proceeded down the center channel that would take them right in front of us. Towing a small rubber dinghy astern, we assumed they had finished their overhaul and were going out on one of their jaunts.

Suddenly, when they were just about abeam of our house, we witnessed some bizarre behavior. Curious, we got out our binoculars. Taking some line, Mr. Higgins-Smythe tied the yacht's tiller in the central position, and then bending down, he opened the floorboards of the cockpit. He then started banging on something and a loud bong, bong, bong echoed around Marigot. A few moments later a geyser of water spouted up into the cockpit. It was easy to see all of this, as we were some two hundred feet above the bay.

We continued to watch, hardly able to believe what was happening. Our two sailors checked their tiller once more, and climbing over the side into their dinghy, they began rowing back into the bay, leaving their sloop putting slowly towards the open Caribbean. Unfortunately, the would-be scuttler's seamanship skills were lacking and the knot securing the yacht's tiller came loose, allowing her to veer off to the right, where she grounded gently on the sand and coral in the shallows to the north side of the bay.

That was enough for Pete and me. We jumped into the Jeep and driving down to the hotel dock, we took our launch out to the grounded yacht. By the time we arrived, Mr. Higgins-Smythe had returned to the boat and climbed back aboard, leaving his wife to wait in their dinghy.

Even though we had enjoyed an unobstructed view of what had taken place so far, we were still finding it hard to believe that this chap was actually trying to sink his boat. The next few minutes, however, would remove any doubts we might have had.

As we came alongside the listing sloop we could see that Mr. Higgins-Smythe was pretty agitated.

"Stand clear, she's going down!" he shouted.

"I wouldn't worry." I replied. "Your boat's only sitting in about six feet of water, she won't go down."

"I said stand clear, you bloody fool." Mr. Higgins-Smythe screamed at us, "I tell you she's going down."

"Look, can we help?" I asked.

"No, I don't want your bloody help." he answered rather rudely, I thought.

He was in the cockpit and kept ducking down below, where he would start banging on something or other before coming back up. It seemed to us that he was trying desperately to get his boat to sink, but he didn't realize that she was already sitting on the bottom and wouldn't go down any further. We guessed that he was breaking off seacock valves, or whatever else he could do to try and sink his little ship, but it was futile.

Pete and I stood off about twenty feet watching the proceedings, and it was obvious each time he came up that he was getting more and more agitated by our presence.

Standing there on his deck, Mr. Higgins-Smythe finally realized that his yacht was not going to sink any further, and so after joining his wife in the dinghy the two of them rowed by, giving us a very dirty look. When Peter and I returned to the shore we told the story to our father, who was greatly amused, and we all went to bed that night shaking our heads at the scuttler's audacity.

Early the next morning, we awoke to a tremendous din. The usual peace and quiet of dawn in Marigot Bay was rudely interrupted by an ungodly racket, "boing, boom, boing" over and over again.

The whole household got up and went to the veranda to see what was causing the clamor. Across the bay, the little red sloop lay on her side. The tide had gone out and she was well and truly stranded. There was a native canoe now alongside her and we could see Mr. Higgins-Smythe with two local fishermen standing on her hull. They were pounding her steel plating with large pickaxes and at every blow a resounding boom echoed around the bay. Unfortunately for them, the sturdy little boat fought on. She was not going to die easily, much to the scuttler's annoyance. After a while, the partners in crime rowed away in the canoe.

Three days later, we had a visit from a bona-fide representative of Lloyds of London, who was investigating a claim for the loss of a little red sloop. We told him what we had witnessed, and he found it hard to believe. Needless to say Mr. Higgins-Smith did not get any insurance money and we subsequently heard that he was being charged with fraud.

A week passed, and while Pete and I were out spear fishing in the outer bay, we came across the bagged mainsail of the sloop drifting across the bottom. Salvaging the sail, we stowed it aboard the *Janeen* and thought no more about it.

Some months later, while anchored in the Berry Islands of the Bahamas, a fishing sloop with an old, patched sail came in and anchored nearby. An idea came to mind. I thought that the little mainsail from the red sloop we had found would fit that fishing boat and it did. We traded the fine little Dacron sail to the happy fisherman for two dozen big lobsters. The lobsters, incidentally, were excellent,

The Bulls of Tarragona

A man sees many things in his life. Some good, some bad, and some of no importance. I am blessed with a good memory and as winter comes to Nova Scotia, I sit near the wood stove and my mind is taken back to the voyages of 1971. I was a deckhand on the 82-foot steel ketch Camelot, and we had made a good passage across the great Atlantic from Antigua to the Azores and onwards into the Eastern Mediterranean and the port of Piraeus, from whence we could carry out our charter cruises.

We spent the summer in the Aegean islands and along the coast of Greece, including a transit of the Corinth canal and a visit to the Dalmatian coast. We saw the wonders of ancient Greece, from the Acropolis in Athens to Cape Sounion, the Temple of Poseidon, and the island of Delos.

On one occasion, we came to the island owned by Stavros Niarchos, the Greek shipping magnate. He was an extremely wealthy shipowner often referred to as the nemesis of Aristotle Onassis. We anchored in a lovely bay near to where Stavros had his palatial home. Anchored in front was his beautiful three-masted schooner *Creole*. The small cove was a beautiful spot with pine trees and a pebble beach. The water was crystal clear and our guests donned swimsuits for a quick swim before cocktails and dinner. I was on deck washing the varnish, as was my duty after each day's sailing, when I noticed a big mahogany speedboat come out from the Niarchos dock.

It was one of those famous Italian classic Riva boats, all varnished and chrome with white leather seats. It sped across the glassy surface of the water throwing up waves of white spray. It appeared to me that they were out for a joyride going nowhere in particular and at one point came quite close to where we were anchored. There were two people aboard, a man and a small boy. The speedboat continued to the other side of the cove where we had anchored but then abruptly came to a stop about 500 yards astern of us. I got the binoculars and had a look at the man in the Riva. He was standing with the engine hatch open looking down into it. He made no move to do anything so I figured it was probably a breakdown he could not repair. I called the captain and the two of us took off in our small launch to see if we could help.

The launch belonging to the *Camelot* was a little ski boat, with the name Lancelot stenciled on the side. We jumped in and sped out to where the varnished launch was drifting. The man appeared to be about 40 years old, with a young boy of seven or eight.

"Do you need a tow?" we asked.

"Yes, tow us over there." he replied, pointing to the rocky point around which his house stood.

It was more of an order than a request, but we put a line on his bow and as we towed the Riva towards his docks, we were feeling pretty good. We had seen the newspapers in Athens and surmised that the man was clearly Stavros Niarchos. Here we were rescuing one of the richest and most famous shipping magnates in the world.

"Yep," I said. "It's Ouzo and rice salad at Stavros' place this evening." I joked to the skipper. After about 30 minutes as we approached the dock in front of the Niarchos mansion, we saw several white uniformed crew in attendance looking out in our direction.

The closer we got to the dock the more agitated Stavros Niarchos became. We finally pulled the Riva alongside just as a group of people came running down from his house, and more in a tender from his yacht *Creole*. They took charge of the Riva speedboat. What happened next could've knocked us down with a feather. We watched in amazement as Mr. Niarchos jumped out of the boat, walked up the dock without a "by your leave," or a word of thanks. He just took off screaming and shouting at his employees. His chief engineer must have gotten his ears burned. Still seated in our little Lancelot we felt a little bit hurt to say the least. We were further insulted by the white uniform guards who were obviously in charge at the dock. The head guy turned to us and motioned with his hands to leave.

All too soon our charter season was over and then it was time to lay a course to the west for Gibraltar where we would fuel up before heading west across the great Atlantic. And so it came to pass that we sailed west along the Spanish coast in October of 1971. Our 82-foot. ketch was bound from the Aegean Sea to the West Indies.

On our westbound journey, we made a stop at the ancient seaport town of Tarragona. It was a beautiful old city dating back to Roman times and our crew walked the streets in awe. I had heard of the bullring and the fighting of the bulls. I resolved that I must see this thing that the Spaniards seemed so passionate about.

After a lunch time bowl of sea food chowder at a waterfront bar, four of our crew walked to the bullring around noon. The bullring is huge and there are hundreds there for the afternoon's entertainment. Somehow, I was reminded of Roman gladiators and the Colosseum. I knew then I would witness a spectacle from ancient times that perhaps would not sit well with me. We bought tickets and sat halfway up the rows. A fanfare signaled the beginning, and the first bull was let into the ring, a proud young black beast with wide curved horns and a high prancing step. With its shoulders held high, it strutted and raced around the ring. Bred to fight and near perhaps 450 kilos it was easily capable of wounding, or even killing a man.

The beginning saw the four banderilleros tease the young bull with their muletas, or capes. Apprentices to the matador, they were clearly fearful, warily staying near to the protective wooden barricades. When the bull rushed, they chanced but one pass of the muleta before seeking shelter, but swallowing their fear they managed to stick three pairs of the flowered sticks into the bull's shoulders. The dance of the toros had begun.

Then the cruel picadors come. They are horsemen with long lances called varas that will break the bull before the matador enters. The bull charges and my friend Sarah, who sat next to me griped my arm. The horses are heavily padded, and the long sharp horns are unable to penetrate. The horsemen however plunged their sharp varas into the bull's back again and again. Soon the proud Toro's shoulder muscles were torn and bleeding, and he was unable to throw his head with any strength. My guts were tensed with the cruelty of it, but I was there and resolved to see the end.

Now the matador entered and with a disdainfully arrogant stride, he made his way to the center of the ring. He alone can wear the suit of lights, gold threaded and sparkling with sequins. The music stirs the blood and there is pass after pass. The red muleta swirls again and again over the blood-drenched sand.

"Ole! Ole! Ole!"

Although strange and horrible to watch, my eyes are riveted on the spectacle below. I take another swig from the open bottle of strong red wine but cannot turn away. Finally, the bull is exhausted, and the toreador prepares the end.

I hear a quiet sobbing to my left and turning I see that Sarah has tears in her eyes.

"Get him," she sobs."

It is only after a few more moments that I realize that she is hoping that the lonely bull will impale the man, but that is not to be. The final thrust of the three-foot long curved sword is clean and pierces the heart. It is over and the bull falls heavily to the ground. The judges in the small box overlooking the ring hang two white handkerchiefs over the edge. The matador has done well and is allowed two ears. I notice that I have tears in my eyes. I will never again go to a bullfight; it is too cruel for me to watch.

The summer passes and finally we're steaming towards Gibraltar along the Spanish coast. I have spent my meager pay advances wisely and I have seen many things of great interest. We have circled the cradle of civilization along the rim of the Mediterranean Sea.

And so, the 82-foot wishbone ketch *Camelot* set sail from Gibraltar on our second Atlantic crossing of the year. After an uneventful passage we made landfall in St. Lucia and Marigot Bay. I signed off then to take a job on another larger sailing vessel. Over the coming months I pondered the adventures of 1971 and our two ocean passages.

Today, a lifetime later, I sit by the fire here in Nova Scotia and often recount tales of adventure to my children Hannah and Jason. But of the bulls of Tarragona, I make no mention, those vivid memories still evoke powerful feelings in my heart that I cannot share.

Janeen under sail bound for Petit St. Vincent and a meeting with a UFO.

"The UFO of Petit St. Vincent"

In January of 1975, we worked our way south during a charter with Barry Goldwater Jr., son of the former U.S. senator and presidential candidate, and our 138-foot Herreshoff schooner reveled in brisk trade wind breezes. The charter was proving a great success. Towards the end of the trip, we sailed to the small idyllic island of Petit St. Vincent (PSV) for a day of reef snorkeling and a picnic on the beach. We were surprised to find five other large charter yachts anchored there because in those days visiting yachts would often find themselves alone.

A beautiful area of crystal-clear turquoise-colored water, the pristine islet was surrounded by a semi-circular coral reef. Petit St. Vincent lay at the southern end of the Grenadine Island chain and was famous for its special beach. The sand had a magical pink hue to it. I suppose this was a result of some unique coral anomaly, but I have never seen it anywhere else in the world.

Our party spent a great day snorkeling over the coral gardens and the chef prepared a succulent lobster salad served with white wine that the guests ate on the beach.

Later that evening back on the *Janeen*, Barry Jr. brought out the toy he had brought from the states. It was a six-foot long box kite with red, blue, and yellow panels. He passed it to me to rig for him, which I did.

By cocktail hour I had it ready and carried it back to the stern, where Mr. Goldwater and his guests were beginning their evening drinks. At the time I owned a huge Vom Hofe tuna fishing reel filled with about 300 yards of heavy line. The reel had been aboard the schooner when she came from California and had the initials Z.G., and Catalina Island Big Game Fishing Club inscribed on the front. I often wondered if it had belonged to the famous western writer, Zane Grey, who was an ardent big game fisherman and a member of the Catalina Fishing Club.

Fastening the reel to one of the heavy aft stanchions, we attached the big kite and sent it aloft. There was a brisk breeze, and it took off upwards like a skyrocket.

After a gourmet dinner in the wardroom, our guests adjourned to the aft deck with the usual liqueurs. They were in good spirits by then and although the kite was still aloft, we could no longer see it. Only the steady pressure on the line was proof that it was still sailing high above the schooner. Mr. Goldwater went over to the rail and looked up.

"I can't see the kite Lou, is it still up there?" he asked.

"Yes, it is," I said, "just feel the line."

Leaning over he took hold of the line and felt the slight but steady vibration.

"You need a light in that thing, Barry." one of his friends commented.

Barry Jr. looked at me questioningly, and I said, "why not?"

We reeled it in and taking a spare life jacket strobe light from the locker, I taped it into the center of the kite. These small lights were only about the size of a pack of cigarettes, but they gave off an extremely bright flash. They were designed so searchers could locate a man in the water at night.

There was still a nice breeze blowing as we sent our little aircraft aloft for the second time. When it had attained the same altitude as before, we went to the stern to have a look. Drifting erratically back and forth over the Petit St. Vincent anchorage, the flashing strobe light produced an eerie effect. At every flash, the colors of the kite could be clearly seen against the darkness of the night sky.

It wasn't long before our flashing aircraft drew the attention of the other yachts. Dinghies and launches soon began running between the boats. We could see the passengers and crew of other vessels standing on deck as they looked up into the night sky at our gaily flashing kite.

"UFO! UFO!" the shouts came from around the anchorage.

Finally, a Zodiac speedboat from the big ketch anchored nearest to us came skidding alongside. A very young English crewman who was almost breathless in his excitement drove it.

"Have you seen it? Look, up there, it's a UFO!" he managed to blurt out between gasps.

We followed his outstretched arm and looking up with grave faces we offered some loud oohs and aahs, playing along with him.

What came next though left us all struggling to control our laughter.

"Yes, it's a UFO." the young fellow in the speedboat repeated, "And the captain of the *Panda* anchored over there, has been in contact with it on the radio. It's going to send down a landing craft soon, so I just came over to warn you. We're alerting everyone in the anchorage."

As he sped off to alert the next yacht, everyone on the *Janeen* burst into fits of laughter, and none of us could remember when we had last shared such a farce. But it wasn't over yet. The finale to this funny episode would secure forever the legend of the Petit St. Vincent UFO.

Twenty minutes after the young English sailor had brought his news, a squall came rolling down on the anchorage bringing gusty winds and the twine holding our kite parted at the reel before we could bring it down. As we looked on our flashing spacecraft took off to the west, disappearing behind the island of Carriacou, never to be seen again. Mr. Goldwater took the loss in good form. It was a pity we missed the frantic confusion that would have surely ensued had the spacecraft been reeled in to land on our stern!

Harbinger under full sail, ghosts down Sir Francis Drake Channel bound for a meeting with Some famous people.

RUMORS

Rumors are a fact of life. Whether you're involved or not, they can often affect our lives in some small way. Whether you read it in a newspaper, see it on television, hear it from friends next door or colleagues at work, rumors circulate. Most are harmless, though some are not. But for the most part, we all get sucked in, to some degree. "Did you hear that....," "You'll never believe what I just saw....," "I didn't know that...." etc. Some may call it just plain gossip, but one thing is for sure, most rumors turn out to be, well, just rumors. Here is a case in point:

During our term on the classic teak ketch *Harbinger*, we spent the winters chartering in the British Virgin Islands. We based the yacht at the Sunsail marina in Soper's Hole, West End, Tortola, the only marina who could handle our deep draft. It was a beautiful location, and we were happy there. The owners of this complex had done a fine job and it was both artistic and well-designed. The *Harbinger* looked very stately positioned at the end of the main "T" dock and there were always a few people wandering down to admire her graceful sweeping hull and classic good looks. In between charters, they would usually find us revarnishing the endless teak, mahogany and cherrywood, or shining up the brass, a seemingly ongoing activity.

On most days, anyone walking down the dock would find our two deckhands, Matt and Jay, hard at work on the deck of the big ketch. They were friendly young fellows, in their twenties, with the usual interests of girls, girls, and girls. They were always discussing the opposite sex and hatching plans about how they could meet this one or that one and invite them out on a date. That winter was a good time for them. Being based at Soper's Hole was a real treat in the sense that we weren't constantly moving from island to island up and down the Caribbean, thus giving them more time to indulge in their favorite pastime.

Matt and Jay handled the results of this seemingly endless pursuit in different ways. Jay fell in love with a new lady every week and would be reduced to a catatonic state not unlike the fictional zombies of Haiti. Unfortunately for the rest of us, his new-found loves were mainly tourists on a one- or two-week vacation, and after their all too short stays, Jay would hit rock bottom and stew in inconsolable misery for days.

Matt, on the other hand, seemed to have the problem of finding someone to fall in love with, which my wife always found surprising. He was good looking, with a happy-go-lucky personality and blond hair to boot. But, for some reason, his efforts seemed to bear less fruit than Jay's, and Matt was the one who was forever hatching some plan to impress the ladies. They were inventive lads, and an opportunity would soon arise which would give them the chance to put into action their most daring plan to date.

Our charter booking office, which was based in Road Town, Tortola, called us one morning telling us that a one-week charter had been booked through a Californian charter agent. The agent wouldn't say who the client was as they were required to keep the identity confidential. However, we were informed that it was a Hollywood VIP. We were all curious, especially Matt and Jay. They tried and tried to find out who it was, but no one knew. So, in the end, Matt devised an audacious plan.

That evening, Matt and Jay went to their local bar in Road Town, called the Lobster Trap, and started putting the word out.

"Yes," they told whoever was listening, "Brad Pitt is chartering the *Harbinger*, starting next week. The yacht is down in Soper's Hole, at the marina. It's the big white hulled one."

As is often the case in small communities, the rumor quickly spread. By noon the following day, word had traveled the length and breadth of Tortola. Brad Pitt was coming to sail on the yacht *Harbinger* which was docked at West End. Young women soon began to appear on the dock next to our vessel, looking expectantly around the decks, as if waiting for something to happen. At this point, S-J and myself knew nothing of what was going on and were surprised by the sudden increase in attention the yacht was receiving. However, Matt and Jay were on the ball and quickly went over to the rail to chat up the girls, each armed with a note pad to write down telephone numbers and brazenly offering to introduce them to Brad when he arrived.

Halfway through the week, S-J and I went into Road Town to collect the charter deposit so we could begin provisioning the yacht for the coming charter. We walked into the office, where we were met with high excitement from Frances, Jo, and Judy, the office staff.

"Oh Lou, aren't you lucky. You're going to have Brad Pitt aboard." Jo exclaimed.

"Oh, is that who's coming?" I asked honestly, surprised by the news. "I didn't know."

They all began laughing. "Ha, ha, you don't have to try and hide it from us, we know."

"Well, you must know more than I do, because it's news to me."

"Lou, you're admirable." Frances said, "I know you have to protect the identity of celebrity clients, but we've heard from a very reliable source that it's Brad Pitt."

"Well, no wonder the dock is full of girls." I said to S-J as we left the office.

When we arrived back at the marina, it was plain to see that the news was out. There were now more than twenty young women alongside the *Harbinger* chatting to Matt and Jay, both of whom had huge Cheshire Cat grins on their faces. Needless to say, not much work was going on. When they saw me returning, they broke away from the girls and came over to help load some of the groceries S-J and I had bought.

Matt looked very sheepish as he met me at the rail.

"Hey, skip, did you know that Brad Pitt is going to be our charter guest?"

"How is it that everybody knew this but us?" I answered.

"Yeah Matt, we know. We were just in the booking office and Jo told us he was coming." S-J said.

Matt looked surprised then and gave out a yelp of joy. "So, it's really true, Brad is coming!" He ran off to tell Jay and they went back to the crowd of girls to fuel the fire some more.

As the day of our charter approached, the steady stream of young women and people visiting our dock increased. At any given time during the day there were a dozen girls coming and going, asking about Brad Pitt. In the evenings, there were more.

One group of young ladies said they had come over from the nearby island of St. Thomas because they heard that Brad Pitt had just brought his sailing yacht in and was staying at the marina, and that he had Tom Cruise and Nicole Kidman aboard with him (the multiplication factor). Matt and Jay continued to talk to the girls, taking scores of phone numbers and arranging dates whenever they could.

The day before the charter, it became very apparent that when our VIP did finally arrive, it was going to be a melee. I wondered if we might be better off boarding him at a more secluded location, so I decided to call the agent in Hollywood to find out what the client wanted to do. Her name was Dorothy MacQue and she was the charter agent to the stars.

"Dorothy, how are you today? This is Captain Boudreau of the *Harbinger*. When Mr. Pitt comes aboard this weekend, there are going to be an awful lot of screaming girls around here. Would you like me to arrange for him to board at some other location?"

"Sorry, did you say you're the captain of the *Harbinger*?" she queried.

"Yes, this is Lou Boudreau, and I am the captain of the *Harbinger*."

"Oh well, there's been some misunderstanding. I booked your yacht for Mr. John Singleton."

"No, we've been told that Brad Pitt is arriving the day after tomorrow."

"No, if you're calling from the *Harbinger*, then you will be having John Singleton, the famous movie maker, not Brad Pitt, the famous actor."

I was convinced now there had been a foul-up somewhere, but I had no idea where. Dorothy McQue and I decided to leave the vessel where it was for boarding and John Singleton and his companion would board the *Harbinger* at the marina. When I got off the phone, I gave the news to S-J and the rest of the crew.

"We're not having Brad Pitt." I told them. "It's John Singleton, the film producer who is coming."

Matt and Jay decided privately that we were hiding the true identity of our guest to clear the docks and so, they continue telling the girls that, as far as they understood, it was Brad Pitt. And so, the ruse continued.

RUMORS

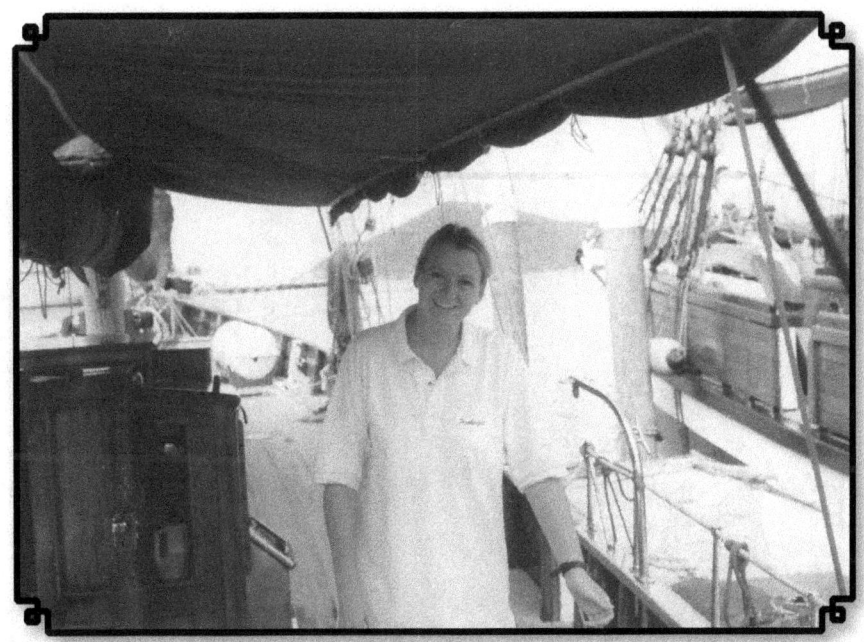

Welcome aboard whoever you are!

At four in the afternoon on embarkation day, Mr. John Singleton and his companion walked down the dock towards the *Harbinger*. Matt and Jay helped with their luggage, and I welcomed them aboard at the gangway. After they were aboard, the two guests settled into the soft cushions on the fantail and S-J served them hors d'oeuvres and champagne.

That evening, there were more passers-by on the dock, and they all walked to the end of the pier to have a peek at our guests sitting on the stern. We heard the same remarks over and over.

"That's not Brad Pitt."

Mr. Singleton became increasingly perplexed, and finally got up and walked over to me. "Captain, how come all these people are mistaking me for Brad Pitt?" So, I told him the story.

During the cruise, Matt and Jay owned up to starting the rumor, "Yup, it was us, skip, but we had no idea it would go quite so far. Trouble was, when you told us the booking office had said Brad Pitt was coming, then we truly believed it ourselves!"

*The crew of the great schooner Sylvania,
Capt. Jeff Thomas to the right in command.
Heroes to be sure.*

"THE LEGEND OF THE SYLVANIA"

A Tale of Heroism on the North Atlantic

The Sylvania was a fine schooner by all accounts. A big vessel at 161 feet, she was one of the famous Indian headers designed by Thomas McManus and built in Gloucester. Her Captain, Jeff Thomas, was well-known along the Gloucester waterfront as a top fisherman and one of the best schooner men alive.

In early August 1918, the *Sylvania* left Yarmouth bound for the banks of Newfoundland to fish for cod and halibut. It was a fair day with a fine southeasterly breeze when Capt. Thomas rounded her up a mile or so off Yarmouth harbor and the crew set sail starting with her main, then foresail, jumbo, and jib. The mate ordered the crew to coil down, and the captain put her on a northeasterly course. Soon the big schooner was rolling slowly to a low swell as she made her way under four lowers.

Her crew were at ease, and they knew that this was the best of times. When all was squared away, they lounged in the lee of the aft deck house, smoked their pipes, and chewed tobacco. They spoke of great catches on the banks of Newfoundland and huge cod that they had jigged there. All experienced men, rugged and hard as only a schooner dory man can be.

Two days passed and the *Sylvania* took a slant away from the land when she was at the latitude of Northern Cape Breton. Some hundreds of miles ahead lay the edge of the great banks of Newfoundland where she was bound. Once there, the skipper Jeff Thomas would either anchor his schooner with a long rope rode or heave too and launch the two-man dories.

It was a scene played out on the Grand Banks a thousand times before. For one hundred years or more, men from the eastern seaboard of Gloucester and Nova Scotia sailed their schooners to what was known as the finest fishing grounds in the world. The schooners were tall sparred and good sailers, able to get to the banks and then return laden with cod, while taking on the worst that the great north Atlantic threw at them. Once the vessels arrived over the shallow banks, the two-man dories would leave the ship and they would row out a few miles to set their baited long lines with 150 hooks or more before standing by for a few hours to give the cod time to bite. During this time, the dory men would unroll their shorter jigging lines and lower them over the side of the dory to jig for cod.

These men knew their trade well and they looked forward to the challenges that lay ahead. There were no men tougher than these. However, unbeknownst to the crew of the *Sylvania*, fate had already set the stage for a deadly challenge against the sea. The crew of the *Sylvania* could not have know that they would be fighting a battle for their lives against the great Atlantic. Hundreds of their fellow dory men over the years and decades had perished in this trade and the situation that was unfolding over the horizon ahead of them would test the brave seamen of the *Sylvania* to the limit, and her crew would need to draw on bravery and strength in the coming days.

It was April 14, 1918, a fateful day to be sure. The dawn broke clear and the weather proved to be holding for yet another fine day at sea. The big schooner was making a fast passage of it to the banks when the forward starboard lookout let out a cry.

"Submarine off to starboard" he called aft.

Capt. Thomas walked quickly forward and put his hand to his brow and peered to the northeast. The rest of the crew followed him to the rail and followed the lookouts raised arm.

Sure enough, a grey hulled submarine was on the surface steaming towards them. Capt. Thomas knew right away that this meant trouble. He walked back to the helm.

"Hold her steady now." he told the helmsman.

"Aye skipper" he said handing a spoke to the starboard.

At perhaps 700 yards, the submarine's forward deck gun barked and a pillar of water rose ahead of the *Sylvania*. It was a

"THE LEGEND OF THE SYLVANIA"

warning shot to be sure, but Capt. Thomas and his crew were left in no doubt as to its meaning.

"Lower away from forward." he shouted.

The brave crew of the *Sylvania* went about their task with great uncertainty in their hearts. They leapt to the sheets and halyards to lower away the sails, as they had done so many times in the past. Many of her brave crew might've guessed that this could be the last time.

With canvas stowed, the *Sylvania* lay rolling in the slow Atlantic swell, her masts tracing a wide arc across the sky. Capt. Thomas ordered a dory launched, and he and two others boarded and rowed to the submarine. The German captain appeared in the conning tower and a brief conversation ensued.

"What is your cargo?" the commander asked.

"We have no cargo, we're bound for the fishing grounds to fish for cod." Capt. Thomas replied.

"I must sink your ship." the German commander stated. "I will give you ten minutes to get off your ship."

Capt. Thomas and his two crew members rowed back to the *Sylvania* and came along her lee side.

"All right boys, they're going to sink her, they've given us ten minutes so grab what you can. Get what water you can and launch two more dories." he ordered.

The crew of the *Sylvania* launched two more dories and loaded them with what meager water and supplies they were able to grab quickly. Then they rowed slowly away from the proud schooner for the last time. They watched as the Germans launched a small boat from a deck hatch and rowed to the *Sylvania*. Some of the submarine's men went aboard and left after perhaps ten minutes. After perhaps another fifteen minutes, Capt. Thomas and his crew heard a massive explosion and the *Sylvania*, a once proud Gloucester schooner was ripped in half and sunk in a matter of moments.

The German submarine turned quickly and made off to the north, where she disappeared from view. Capt. Thomas and his brave crew were in four dories, and he knew that the chances of seeing land again were slim. He knew that hundreds and hundreds of brave seamen had perished at sea through bad weather, storms, and wrecks. He also knew that pitting his dories against the sea with his brave crew would be a hard fight to win. But the captain was a schooner man, a brave strong man and he would not go down without a fight.

Taking the cover off the dory compass box, Thomas laid a rough course for Cape Breton Island. It would be no easy task, for what wind there was albeit light was from the south, and the men would pull against it.

"There's nothing for it, boys, we must pull slow and steady if we're to make landfall." the skipper told his crew.

And so began a battle of men against the sea, a battle played out so many times before, with sad endings. The men picked up their oars and began to row. The three dories lay spread out over a rolling sea, with more than 200 miles between them and land. Capt. Thomas was under no illusions. He knew this would be the test of his lifetime. The dory men tried to keep the dories within 100 feet of each other and every few hours they stopped so the men could eat some bread or dried biscuit and drink out of a small barrel of water.

The sun set to the west of them beneath a cloudy sky. All hands were cold by now and tiredness had begun to set in, but there would be no solace. They faced only hardship and misery. But these were the dory men of Gloucester and Nova Scotia; tough hardy men.

The night passed and all hands were grateful to see the sun rise slowly in the east. The wind had held light and a low swell rolled in from the north. The rising sun offered a modicum of warmth to the men, but it was still cold for the most part.

Capt. Thomas pulled his watch from his vest pocket and popped the top. It was 8 o'clock in the morning.

He signaled for the dories to come close together and they passed a line from bow to stern

"I'm sorry boys, but there's nothing for it, we must row or there will be widows in Gloucester and Yarmouth if we fail." he told them with a tear in his eye. He knew that every hour in the dories lessened their chances, and he knew many of the wives and families of his crew, but Capt. Thomas was great schooner man, and he would lead them to the end.

The men ate sparingly of the remaining biscuit and bread and drank some water. Then Capt. Thomas ordered the lines cast off again, the dories drifted abreast of each other, and on that unforgiving North Atlantic Sea, the brave crew of the *Sylvania* marshalled what remaining strength they had and began to pull again. Few words were spoken as all knew there was nothing much to say. By late afternoon, the wind rose abaft the beam of the dories and although it gave the *Sylvania* men an easier slant to pull against, the sea rose slightly and spray began coming over the rails, so the dories and the men became wet, thus doubling their suffering.

By evening of the second day, Thomas and his crew knew that there was trouble ahead. The men tried to take turns at the oars, while some took their time off trying to sleep in the bottom of the dories. This proved impossible as the men were wet and uncomfortable. But some fell asleep through sheer exhaustion. Most had blistered hands and others had cuts across their palms where the oar handles had worn the skin. The suffering of the *Sylvania* men that night was great, and as they shivered, they thought of their wives and families over the sea ahead of them.

There was a full moon that night. Capt. Thomas could see his crew huddled over the oars or laying in the bottom of the boat and, although he was sympathetic, he was tired as well. Through the early morning hours, the wind blew stronger, and the waves grew higher. The breaking crests looked eerily white in the moonlight as they broke to windward of the dories.

Just before dawn the third day the lead dory took a wave on her beam and rolled over, throwing four men into the sea. The other two dories backed water and pulled over to the capsized boat. They pulled the men aboard and the remaining two dories took two men each. Capt. Thomas looked at the swamped boat and realized that it would be pointless to try and bail it out, as the waves washed over it. In any case, the oars had gone and were nowhere to be seen. And so, on the last day, two heavily laden dories pulled once more towards Cape Breton.

And so, the brave captain and crew of the *Sylvania* started their third day in the dories rolling towards Cape Breton Island.

Sylvania news clip

The exhausted crew were near death and could hardly pull on their oars and the fact that they had any strength left at all was a testament to their hardiness and stamina.

Finally, towards noon on the third day, they saw a dark smudge on the horizon to the west.

"Land ahead boys" shouted Capt. Thomas and every man turned to see the low distant hills.

By early afternoon, they knew for sure that land was ahead, and the men drew some final reserves from their aching cold bodies to take up the blood-stained handles of the oars one last time. By late afternoon, the utterly exhausted crew of the *Sylvania*, led by their brave Capt. Thomas made landfall in a rocky cove in Cape Breton. There were homes there, and after walking to the closest one, they were soon seated next to a roaring fire.

And so ended one of the great struggles of men against the sea. Capt. Thomas and all the *Sylvania* crew survived the ordeal. The skipper and crew had fought against all odds and done the impossible. Certainly, lesser men would've failed, but these men were dory men and tougher, stronger men you would not find. Their story became legend along the waterfronts of the eastern seaboard and the Canadian Maritimes and the name *Sylvania*, along with the names of her captain and crew, were spoken with respect.

It will be noted that the crew list of the schooner *Sylvania* held the names Devine and Boudreau. We, their descendants, salute them now. They were great men.

Lou standing near the wreck of the Cita.

WRECKERS

Wrecking is an age-old occupation usually relegated to dubious characters from bygone eras. When I hear the word wrecker my mind conjures up visions of fog bound shores with folks in woolen sweaters, carrying booty up the cliffs from a square-rigger stranded on the rocks below. Or a picture of tropical shores and a pirate hanging a lantern in a coconut tree to lure the ship down on the reef. I remember the legend of Sam Lord, a man of some doubtful integrity who lived in Barbados in the years of yore.

> On this little island lived a buccaneer, Sam Lord was his name,
> He wrecked all the vessels,
> Laden down with treasure,
> Sailing from the Spanish Main,
> He used to hang the lanterns in the coconut trees,
> And lure the ships down on the reef,
> Oh, when the sailors thought they sighted land,
> Alas, they also ran aground,
> Well, he buried his treasure so deep in the ground,
> Till this day, it has never been found,
> People may search from time to time,
> His fortune they will never find.

I believed the tradition of wrecking to be a part of history or at the very least a dim memory in the mind of an old islander in a woolen jumper on some faraway shore. Surprisingly, the winter of 1997 would find us taking part in this legally questionable activity.

My wife, Sarah-Jayne's ancestral home is in the storied Isles of Scilly, and we found ourselves spending the winter of 1997 there. This tiny archipelago is located some twenty-eight miles from Lands

End in Cornwall, England, and is made up of five inhabited islands, surrounded by a selection of reefs, ledges, smaller islands, and jagged rocks, daunting enough to strike fear into the stoutest of seafaring hearts. Prone to fog and gales, these misty shores are steeped in the legends of shipwrecks.

Sitting at the hub of sea trade routes, which have been used since ancient times, the shoals surrounding the Isles of Scilly are littered with the bones of ships, both great and small. The notable Thomas W. Lawson's bones lie there. Even today, the most modern navigational aids cannot prevent Scilly's granite teeth from extracting their toll from passing ships, although they are far more infrequent these days.

Great tides, treacherous currents, and misty fogs can make this a foreboding place. Yet, this rugged group of small islands also has a stunning and natural beauty. When the weather is fine, you can wonder at the picturesque views, the numerous white beaches, and crystal-clear waters passing in between. On a clear day, if you stand up on the hill of the garrison you can see Bishop Rock, the tallest lighthouse in the world proudly standing guard. Further around to the west, the seas can be seen breaking over the Western Rocks, throwing white spray into the air.

The Scillonians, who inhabit the island, are friendly characters, who have a long history of wrecking and they have a special prayer concerning ships passing by their islands.

> *"Whilst we do not pray for shipwrecks, oh Lord, but should a wreck occur, we ask that thou wilt guide it to the Isles of Scilly, for the benefit of its poor inhabitants."*

That prayer was answered in 1997. On March 25th of that year, the 3,000-ton container ship *Cita* left Southampton, England bound for Belfast, Ireland with a cargo of 145 containers holding general cargo worth millions of pounds. That evening, the fog closed in surrounding the islands. By the early hours of the following morning, a message was received from the *Cita*, reporting that she had taken the ground at Newfoundland Point on St. Mary's, the largest of the islands. Scilly had claimed yet another victim.

Her entire crew was taken off safely by the local lifeboat in the early hours of the morning. Sometime afterwards, the *Cita* slowly rolled over onto her side, dumping somewhere between eighty and one hundred of her containers into the sea. The tides then kindly deposited many of them high and dry along the many coves and bays of these islands.

True to tradition, it didn't take the islanders very long to sound the alarm. Church bells rang and word quickly spread, "Wreck! There be a wreck down at Newfoundland Point" people shouted, knocking on doors. Word soon arrived at "Aurgia," the home of my mother-in-law, Jeanne Reseigh, and where S-J and I happened to be staying at the time. Jeanne yelled up the stairs, "Get your skates on you two, we're off wrecking!"

By the time we had gotten our coats on, Jeanne was revving the car engine outside the front door. As we drove along, we met cars going this way and that way. Each time we stopped to chat through the car window we were informed of a different location where containers had been washed ashore, and what kind of cargo it held.

"There's shorts and shirts at Deep Point." or, "A couple of containers of children's clothes are sitting in Porthcressa Bay." or "There's a whole container of sneakers down at Watermill Cove."

It was just like the film *Whisky Galore!* and Scillonians soon began plundering the *Cita's* cargo from the containers that had been dutifully washed ashore. The island was buzzing with activity and excitement, but there was no fighting between the islanders, and many were ready to help others get something. Joseph, my wife's cousin, was standing in one of the containers helping to pass out boxes of shirts. By the time he had emptied the container, he noticed that every box had been hauled off and there was not one left for him! However, some kind fellow gave him a couple of his own boxes.

There were containers holding mahogany doors, car tires, computer hard drives. Some held golf bags, barbecue sets and rolls of fabric. Others held wooden plate racks, power tools, batteries, and bathroom accessories. There was a huge amount of tobacco, which unfortunately sat in their canvas bags drenched in salt water. There were even several forklift trucks! The booty was incredible and John Hicks, another of my wife's cousins, remarked it was as good as winning the lottery.

As the day wore on it became apparent that there was more booty than even the resourceful Scillonians could manage. Much of it was dry and had not been damaged at all, but some were awash in the sea and would have to be dried out. The booty was collected and swiftly deposited into the homes sprawled around the island. Barns and garages were filled with tires and some of the larger items. Golf bags were stowed into closets, whether they had golf clubs to put in it or not. It didn't matter if you weren't a golfer, this was wrecking, and you could always dispose of it later (or take up golf).

A contingent of mainland police constables arrived on the *M/V Scillonian* and stationed themselves at the various places where most of the loot seemed to be coming from. Surprisingly, they weren't there to stop the islanders from liberating the cargo (except the tobacco) but were there to hand out the Wreck and Salvage forms to them as they dragged their loot up the paths. These were meant to be completed by each wrecker, stating what they had managed to salvage–for record only, of course! One local constable, who happened to be stationed near the container holding car tires was heard to remark "If I catch anyone with bald tires on their vehicle after next week, I intend to book them for laziness!"

In life, there is always the green-eyed monster waiting in the wings somewhere, and this monster circulated in various newspapers and reports around England, accusing the islanders of just plain old "looting" and having no concern but to fill their own pockets. I suppose those living on the English mainland would naturally feel this way, but I wonder how many of them would have joined in the "rampage" had they themselves been on St. Mary's at the time? The other view held is that the islanders did a tremendous service by clearing up all the debris and mess which had littered their picturesque island. However, it wasn't only the islanders who benefited from this accident. A group of ladies, who with the assistance of many other locals, gathered up armfuls of children's clothing, washed, dried, and got them ready to send to Romania and Africa to help the children there.

The High Barbaree dips her lee rail in a strong gust leaving St. Thomas harbor headed for West End and Pirates Gold.

OF PIRATE'S GOLD

As a Nova Scotia sea captain, I should know something about pirate's treasure. Oak Island in Mahone Bay is a place steeped in legend. But let's put legend aside for a moment and I'll tell you a real treasure story. In my wandering days as a West Indies-based captain, I had some firsthand treasure experience.

The buccaneers of long ago had a habit of stashing their loot in the oddest places and every year there's a new story from some faraway shore of treasure found. The history of the British Virgin Islands is steeped in legends of pirates and buried treasure. This string of small islands, bays, and sandy cays was the perfect hideaway for buccaneers and many of their names hark back to the days of "Pieces of Eight" on the Spanish Main. Deadman's Bay, Dead Chest Island, Jost van Dyke, and Bluebeard's Castle are all reminiscent of an era when a cutlass in a strong man's hand was the law.

The Virgin Islands provided an excellent locale for the swift privateers. The long stretch of water known as Sir Francis Drake Channel is like an inland sea, offering numerous anchorages where a schooner or brig could find a safe haven. Large natural harbors such as the bight at Norman Island (the real Treasure Island), Road Harbor on Tortola, West End, and Great Harbor on Peter Island must have been just as attractive to the old-time sailors as they are to yachtsman today. A two-hundred-ton schooner with a good skipper and crew could easily sail to and from their anchorage in these harbors.

With all the loot that these dubious characters were hauling in, they were always on the lookout for a safe place to hide it and the many uninhabited bays and coves of the Virgin Islands provided this. The sands of time have run, and scores of years have passed, but many of the secrets of that bygone era remain.

It is not surprising then, that from time-to-time tourists visiting the Virgin Islands turn up the odd gold doubloon or gold chain. The government of the islands long ago recognized this source of lucre and declared any treasure found in the territory of the islands to be the property of the government.

In May of 1989, the Johnsons arrived in West End, Tortola for a week-long charter on the *High Barbaree*, our seventy-eight-foot Philip Rhodes ketch. There were five in the family, three of them young daughters. They were a few hours early, so as we carried their luggage aboard, I suggested they have a walk around the bay while we finished our preparations. We were on a twenty-four-hour turn around and every free minute was precious.

There had been great plans over the years to deepen the head of West End harbor and now finally it was being done. A huge dredge sucked up tons of sand and ground up coral from the bottom of the bay and spit it out on the shore. There were huge piles of sand there, full of seashells of many different types.

Mrs. Johnson expressed an interest in shell collecting and I felt that they might find a good selection in the sand piles,

"If you like shell collecting, then just walk along the beach to the sand piles over there and you'll probably find plenty." I suggested.

"That sounds like a great idea. We'll go and do that while you finish getting ready." she replied.

The week turned out well and our party seemed to enjoy themselves even more than usual. We took them snorkeling by Dog Rocks and explored the white sand beaches of Anegada. I took them fishing in the launch and we caught yellow tail snapper for the table. The weather held and we had several glorious sailing days and our big steel ketch reveled in the trade wind breezes. All too soon for the Johnsons, the cruise came to an end, and we sailed into Beef Island on their final night.

The following morning, they left to catch a flight to San Juan where they would connect for the United States. My crew was very happy with the gratuity they left, a full fifteen percent. As the captain, I didn't usually accept gratuities as a matter of policy, and I didn't expect anything on this occasion. However, after my guests had gone ashore and I went into my cabin, I found a brown envelope waiting for me. It was sticking out from under my pillow, and as I picked it up, I almost dropped it, it was so heavy. Opening it I found a note and a small package wrapped in tin foil. Curious, I quickly read the note.

Dear Captain Lou,

Our thanks once again to you and your crew for a wonderful cruise. Just how wonderful you could never have imagined. Remember the first day in West End, when you told us to go and look for shells in the sand pile? Well, we picked up some rather pretty shells, but that wasn't all we found. Robin spotted what looked like a huge flat abalone shell, but it had a shiny part to it. When I lifted it out of the sand it weighed a ton, and I could hardly hold it. When we took a closer look, we couldn't believe our eyes, because there was a clump of gold coins, Lou, all fused together by time and coral. They must have been in a bag that had fallen into the bay many years ago - I wonder how many? Anyway, they must have been dredged up for us to find. We didn't say anything to you before, as we weren't sure how you would react.

So, thank you for showing us where to find that small piece of treasure. Maybe you should go back and look for yourself. In the meantime, we want you to have these two coins in our appreciation.

It was signed by the Johnsons, and as I slowly opened the tin foil, I found myself looking at two large gold coins, my share of the West End treasure. What's that old saying? "Finders keepers, losers weepers?" Well, I agree!

Sarah with Unicorn's forecourse in the background.

The Romance of the Sea

We've all heard about the romance of the sea. You know, Humphrey Bogart and his schooner *True Love*, Errol Flynn and his schooner *Zaca*, and others famous characters whose romantic escapades were linked to beautiful ladies and fine schooners. And yes, it happened to this Nova Scotia Sea captain as well. So read on dear reader, here is my tale.

I left the fair Nova Scotia coast in 1952 when I was but one year old. My first voyage to the West Indies was on the schooner *Doubloon*, which along with the *Yankee* and *Windbloweth* made up Nova Scotia Windjammer Cruises, this province's first windjammer cruise business owned and operated by my father Capt. Walter Boudreau. I went to sea at age 16, and followed in my father's footsteps, eventually becoming a sea captain.

My lifestyle hadn't really lent itself to marriage. Being a sea captain just didn't allow me a permanent residence. I was always on the go, traveling from one side of the ocean to the other. Even if I was lucky enough to meet a prospective girlfriend, I was usually planning to sail off to some distant land the next day, unable to secure more than one date. Not exactly a recipe for success.

However, I can't blame my occupation entirely. I must confess to being one of those guys - I wonder how many of us are out there - who have that certain inability to interact easily with the opposite sex. In the company of girls, I always stuttered, conversation was usually staccato, and on those occasions when I dared go to a party, I usually hid behind the nearest door in the hopes that no one would ask me to dance. I had no dancing rhythm whatsoever, which was strange because I was an excellent guitar player. I knocked things over when normally I wasn't clumsy. For some unknown reason, women just seemed to scare the daylights out of me, and I was afraid I'd never marry because I'd never find a woman I wasn't terrified of.

By the latter part of 1993, at the tender age of 42, I still hadn't resolved this problem, and my parents were particularly worried about my state of (non) affairs. However, little did I know that my future had already taking a new course.

It is amazing how one seemingly insignificant act can change your whole destiny. The wheels of my destiny had begun turning without my knowing it, three months before in England.

A young English girl was living in the heart of London, working for a perfume company. Thoroughly fed up with her high-pressure job and city life, she was looking for a change. She loved to travel and was hoping to get away from her frantic London existence to find adventure elsewhere.

One Monday morning, while on her way to the office, she picked up a couple of the freebie magazines stacked by the entrances to the London Underground train system. On this day, however, she picked up one magazine she had never bothered to pick up before, and one which she really had no interest in. It was aimed at the Australians and New Zealanders living in London.

Flicking through the pages, she noticed a tiny three-line advert.

"SAILING IN THE CARIBBEAN. Four-month trip on a sailing yacht round the West Indies. Beginners welcome."

Intrigued, she phoned the number and spoke to the skipper's father. He explained that the 52-foot sloop *Venture*, would begin her next voyage in January of 1994. Deciding to go for it, she paid the fee, gave up her job and flat, and booked a flight to St. Lucia where she would join the *Venture*.

Meanwhile, I was skippering the 140-foot brig *Unicorn*, running cruises up and down the coast of St. Lucia. It was a day job, at work by 7:00 a.m. and home by 10:00 p.m. The trips were fun, and we usually had an interesting bunch aboard. Sometimes, on a good day, we had as many as one hundred and twenty-five people crowding the decks of the brig.

One morning in January 1994, I was sitting on the stern of the *High Barbaree*, my home at the time, when I saw the yellow hull of the *Venture* sail into Marigot Bay. Skippered by my long-time friend, Roger, it wasn't long before he came over in his dinghy to say hello. We agreed to meet at the Shack restaurant that evening for a round of drinking. He had arrived to pick up his new crew, before embarking on a four-month voyage around the islands, and down to Panama and back.

One of the crew was a lovely English girl named Sarah-Jayne. Tall and slim with blonde hair and blue eyes, it was her smile that really captivated me. Whenever she smiled at me it was pure magic and my heart would miss a beat...or two...I lost count.

The evening passed all too quickly, and Roger took his crew back to the *Venture*. They were leaving the following day for Panama and wouldn't be returning to St. Lucia for a couple of months. Although I hadn't had the chance to talk much to Sarah-Jayne, I shook her hand and told her I hoped to see her again.

"That would be nice." she said, smiling that smile of hers and putting my heart into cardiac arrest. After she had gone, I boldly confided to the bartender that I was going to marry her.

"Best you check wid' she first." he cautioned me, "Women don't like men to tell them what to do when it comes to marrying."

They sailed out to the west the following morning and I went into Castries to join the *Unicorn* for my daily tourist run down the coast.

As February drew to an end, I found myself scanning the westward horizon for the *Venture's* yellow hull. Sure enough, one afternoon I spotted her sailing toward St. Lucia. I was elated; I couldn't wait to get a glimpse of Sarah-Jayne and kept peering through the binoculars.

On this particular day we had one hundred thirty-four passengers aboard and we were already abeam of La Toc Bay, headed for our home port, where our guests would disembark at the end of their cruise. They were already stuffing their towels and suntan lotion back into their beach bags and were surprised when I turned the *Unicorn* sharply away from the land towards the approaching *Venture*.

Morella, our hostess on *Unicorn*, took it upon herself to make a public service announcement.

"Ladies and gentlemen, may I have your attention, please. Don't be alarmed, our captain is in love and his girlfriend is on that little yellow boat up ahead. He's just going to wave to her before we head back to Castries."

Much to my embarrassment, our passengers erupted into applause and began to cheer. I suppose no one can resist a good romantic tale, and obviously, they appreciated mine. I swung the *Unicorn* by the *Venture* at less than 100 feet and waved to Sarah-Jayne who was standing in the cockpit. We gave each other a toot on the horn.

After our passengers disembarked, I raced to Marigot Bay and jumped into my dinghy. I finally met Sarah-Jayne and invited her out for a trip on the *Unicorn* the next day. During the cruise, she told me about her trip to Panama and we talked about our pasts and plans for the future. For the first time in my life, I felt totally at ease with a girl who I wanted to be with. By the end of the cruise, I was in love.

The following day I was planning to invite S-J out to dinner, but when I returned to Marigot in the early evening the *Venture* was gone. I couldn't believe it and for the next couple of days I went about my work like a bear with a sore head. I couldn't get her out of my mind, and I thought I had seen the last of my fair English girl. Just my luck.

Fortunately, three days later, I spotted the yellow hull sitting at the north end of the island. The following day was a Sunday, and I grabbed a taxi to Rodney Bay. Sure enough, the *Venture* was there, anchored in the middle of the harbor. I tried to contact them by radio but had no luck. I had no dinghy, but I couldn't wait any longer. I ran to the marina shop, bought a card, and wrote a note asking if she would like to go to lunch with me. I found Marcus, one of the local guys, and paid him to row out to the *Venture* and hand the card to S-J.

It just so happens that the crew of the *Venture* were on their way ashore when Marcus rowed over to them asking if they "had a Sarah-Jayne aboard?" He gave her the note and, as they came alongside the dock, she was waving the card. As a first date I took Sarah-Jayne for a day sail on the *Unicorn*.

The rest, as they say, is history. S-J left St. Lucia the next day, but she came back out to visit me a month later. For more than two years we sailed the 117 ft. ketch *Harbinger* around the islands of the Caribbean. In the wee hours one morning in December 1995, as the

Harbinger sailed toward the island of Antigua, I asked S-J to be my wife. We were married six months later.

S-J and I sailed the oceans for three years before we gave up the sea and settled back in Nova Scotia where it all began. We live on the south shore now with our two wonderful kids, Jason, and Hannah. For me, life has come full circle. The places and things I left here all those years ago, are still here. But now, as I tell our children my tales of adventure on the sea, my first mate, S-J, is still at my side, another adventurous spirit touched by the romance of the sea.

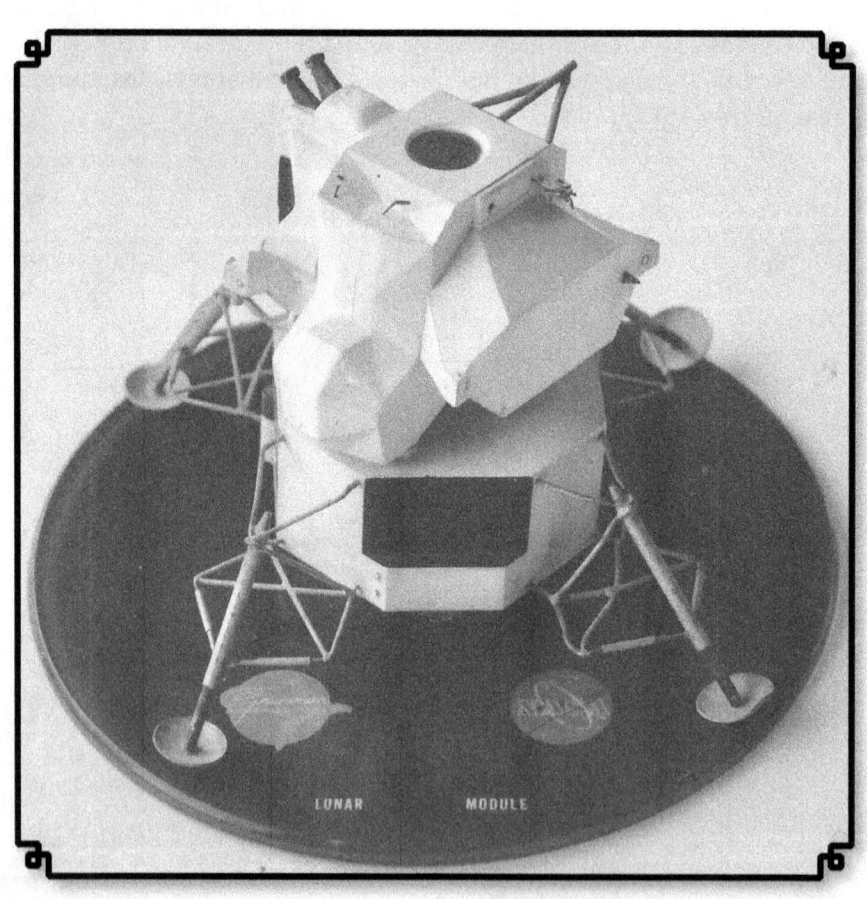

The model of the Lunar Module given as a gift from the astronauts who walked on the moon.

The Men on the Moon and the Secret Lagoons of Marigot Bay

Back in the 1950s, there was a family living in some secret lagoons in the Windward Islands of the West Indies. There was a small hotel on the shores of these lagoons called the Yacht Haven Hotel. It was built by my father, Capt. Walter Boudreau, a pioneer in the windjammer sailing charter business.

The lagoons of Marigot Bay on the west coast of St. Lucia comprised inner and outer bays with a magical sand spit punctuating the two. There was something secret and enchanting about the place. The inner lagoon was surrounded by mangrove trees and the water was crystal clear and light blue to the bottom.

It was here in these enchanting lagoons that my father chose to build his small beach hotel with cottages. It quickly became known for its beauty and charm and many a famous guest visited the enchanted lagoons of Marigot during this era.

It was here that the Boudreau's were raising their five children. For them, they lived the magic of the bay and one of their earliest adventures was waking up one morning to the sight of a twenty-foot-tall pink snail on the beach in front of their home. Of course, it was actually a prop from a film *Dr. Doolittle*, starring Rex Harrison.

Soon, there were many other notable folks, including a visit from the astronauts who just walked on the moon for the first time. They had been sent to the quiet bay to unwind following their walk on a distant moon, and they were also taken for a sail on my father's schooner, *Janeen*, a beautiful 130-foot black-hulled beauty.

I can remember speaking to our gardener, Simon, a man of great wisdom and knowledge. When I said to him that the men who were visiting us just walked on the moon, Simon replied, "Lou, what they want with the moon? Leave it, it's the moon. It will always be there."

And so, the astronauts gave us a gift of a model of the lunar module. It sits on our dining room table overlooking the shore of our home in Nova Scotia. To most, it is naught but an old model. But to me, it reminds me of a time long past when I lived in the magical blue lagoons of Marigot Bay. It reminds me of sailing on my father's schooners in the islands, and the people I met back in those times. And then as I reach out and touch my model of the lunar module and look up at the full moon there in the clear night sky, I am reminded that the gift that was given to me was from men who had walked on another world, and of the kindness they shared with me through the gift of the module.

And then I must leave the room as I feel a tear come to my eye. The memory of a small momentary incident a lifetime ago passes and I retire to my bedroom to sleep a restful night.

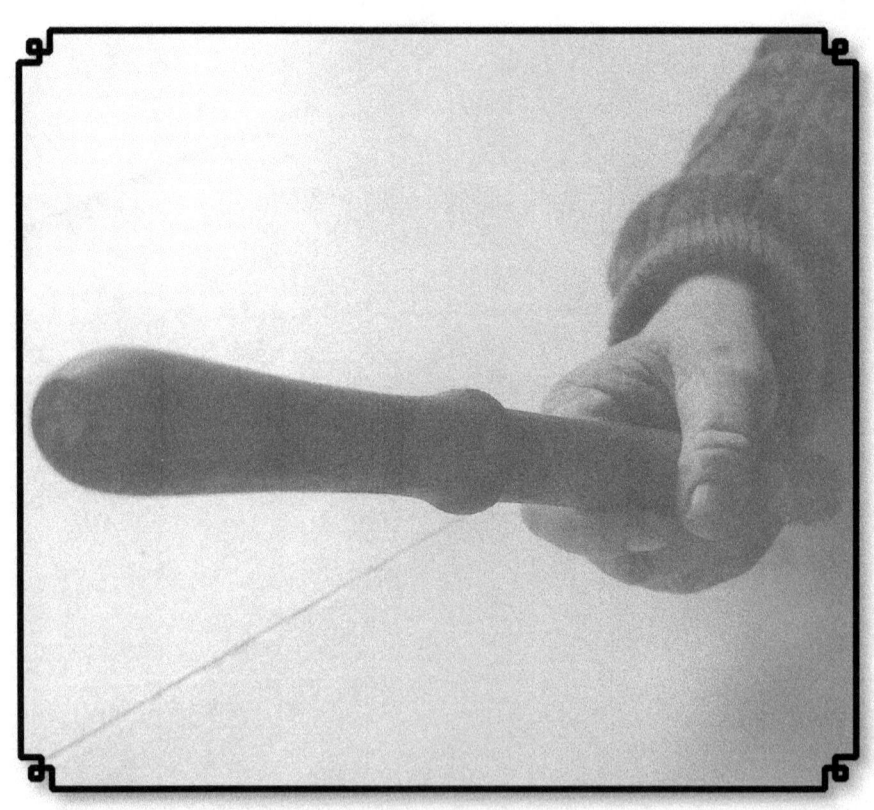

I hold a belaying pin from the Samson, one of the mystery ships.

MYSTERY OF THE SEA

The Sinking of the Titanic and the mystery ships

The sea holds many mysteries. From the infamous captain of the *Flying Dutchman* whose ship and crew are doomed to remain at sea forever because he made a deal with the devil to other mysteries hiding along the reefs of many a hidden cove or shoal. Some of these mysteries tell tales of sunken gold and ships that disappeared beneath the waves only to be discovered a hundred years later.

Here in Nova Scotia, we have our own share of mysteries of the sea. Possibly the most famous is the mystery of Oak Island where despite decades of digging the island still holds it secrets. Did pirates hide a trove there? The question remains unanswered.

Other underwater mysteries remain unsolved. The wreck of the famed schooner *Yankee* that sailed around the world three times lies in the Bras d'Or Lakes where the reason for her sinking still has not been solved. The bays and coves of Mahone Bay harbor many a secret. Some of these tales of mystery are rather mundane at first glance but in fact all carry some interesting story as to how they came to rest at their location.

The *Titanic* sinking is one such Atlantic tragedy, aspects of which are still debated to this day. She hit an iceberg in the early morning hours of Sunday, April 15, 1912, in the North Atlantic Ocean, four days into her first voyage from Southampton to New York City. She was the largest ocean liner in service at the time and had an estimated 2,200 people aboard when she hit an iceberg resulting in the deaths of more than 1,500 people, making it one of the deadliest peacetime maritime disasters in history.

The Titanic had previously received a number of radio warnings of sea ice on April 14th, but she was traveling at more than 22 knots when her lookouts sighted a large iceberg. Unable to turn quickly enough, the *Titanic* suffered a brutal hit that buckled her starboard side steel plating and opened six of her sixteen compartments to the sea (the forepeak, all three holds, and boiler rooms five and six). The *Titanic* had been designed to stay afloat with four of her forward compartments flooded but no more, and the crew soon realized that the ship would sink. They used distress flares and radio messages to get help as some of the passengers were put into lifeboats.

In accordance with existing practice, *Titanic's* lifeboats were designed to carry some passengers to nearby rescue vessels, but not to carry everyone aboard so with the ship sinking rapidly and help still hours away, there was no escape for many of the passengers and crew. Further it was said by many survivors that poor management of the abandon ship process meant that many boats were launched before they were completely full.

The *Titanic* sank with over a thousand passengers and crew still aboard. Almost all those who jumped or fell into the water drowned or died within minutes due to the effects of cold shock and incapacitation. A nearby ship named *Carpathia* arrived about an hour and a half after the sinking and rescued the last of the survivors by 9:15 a.m. on April 15th, some nine and a half hours after the collision. The disaster shocked the world and caused widespread outrage over the lack of lifeboats, lax regulations, and the unequal treatment of the three passenger classes during the evacuation. Subsequent inquiries recommended sweeping changes to maritime regulations, leading to the establishment in 1914 of the International Convention for the Safety of Life at Sea (SOLAS).

There were however some mysterious circumstances that to this day remain a matter of debate. I refer to the three ships called the mystery ships. These were ships either sighted by the *Titanic* or possibly other vessels involved in the rescue. To this day stories referring to the mystery ships are still being debated. Why did these vessels whichever ones they were not go to the rescue of the *Titanic* but instead disappeared into the mist? One theory is that one or more of these vessels were carrying illegal loads of rum from the French islands of Saint Pierre Miquelon, while the other more plausible theory in the debate is that one or more vessels had another type of illegal cargo which may have been seals. One of these ships was called the *Samson*. Originally the vessel used by Admiral Byrd in his expedition to the Antarctic, she was a three-masted schooner with a smokestack and powered by a steam engine. It is said that she arrived days later in Iceland where a load of illegal seal was unloaded.

Later *Samson* was named the *City of New York* under the ownership and command of the famous Captain Lou Kennedy of Nova Scotia. He used the ship as a multipurpose cargo vessel between the West Indies and Nova Scotia. She often had a cargo of salt onboard from the Turks and Caicos that would be used in Nova Scotia's salt cod industry. My father Walter Boudreau sailed with captain Kennedy and my father had such great respect for Lou Kennedy and his seagoing skills that when I was born, I was named Lou after Lou Kennedy

As shown in the photograph, I am holding a belaying pin given to me as a gift by the son of Jeff Thomas, a very famous Gloucester schooner captain and inscribed with the name City of New York on the wooden shaft.

It is indeed a remarkable link that my family has with the *City of New York* previously known as the *Samson*, one of the mystery ships.

Occasionally I walk to the waterfront in Mahone Bay, and I stand on the stones looking out to the great Atlantic. Then I look down at the large belaying pin I am holding in my hands. A strange feeling comes over me and I tremble slightly. If this wooden bit of sailing ship rigging could talk what a strange tale it would tell. The *Titanic* hitting the iceberg, the people dying in the icy ocean, the mystery ships, and the ship from which my belaying pin came.

Indeed, the great Atlantic is filled with many a strange mystery the answers to which will never be known.

I turn to walk back to my home on the hill and the belaying pin in my hands seems strangely alive. Passersby see an old sea captain with a tear in his eye. They cannot know that I have just glimpsed a moment in time long ago when mystery drifted over the North Atlantic.

The Ramona ghosts out of the lee of St. Vincent bound for Port Elizabeth Bequia, where she will meet a bombardment of rum bottles.

OPERATION RUM BOTTLE

(As told by my father, Captain Walter Boudreau)

I sailed the *Ramona* from San Diego through the Panama Canal and back to the island of St. Lucia. Joel stayed with me, and I began to groom him to take over the schooner from time to time, leaving me more time to spend with my family. He was a reliable young man and an excellent seaman.

Within a few months, there came about the first of many interesting episodes that put our little hotel firmly on the map. Frank Jameson was a mover. He was one of those individuals who made things happen. He was well-connected politically in the U.S., and a millionaire in his own right. As president of a company supplying the military with missiles, he often dealt with the top brass of the army, navy, and air force, as well as senators and congressmen. He liked to tell everyone about his little hotel in paradise and the schooner yacht that was kept moored there. He was a tall, well-built man with a booming voice and a kind heart. He never once visited the island without a present for each of the kids. We were very fond of him.

Frank began sending some of his sophisticated friends down to Marigot to stay at the hotel. Terry and I were not overly thrilled about this, because the Yacht Haven was not really set up as a luxury establishment. It was the early days of tourism in St. Lucia and the infrastructure was still fairly primitive. Our phone worked only sporadically, and we shut off the power from our generators at twelve o'clock every night. Although a route had been bulldozed to the bay from the main road, it was still unsurfaced, becoming muddy and impassible in heavy rains. All in all, it was not the kind of island getaway to send clients who were accustomed to the Ritz. Anyway, Frank persisted and would phone Terry to say that senator so and so and his wife would be arriving in two days time, and in three days, to expect General Peabody and his wife, and to please take good care of them.

On one particular evening, he called Terry and told her to have the *Ramona* ready and the hotel on "code red alert" because some very important guests would be arriving soon. He said he was really going to put Marigot Bay on the map this time. There would be a group of twenty or more senators, congressmen, admirals, generals, and even Mendel Rivers, coming to Marigot. Also included in the group would be the chairman of the Joint Chiefs of Staff of the U.S. military. They were to begin arriving in Martinique by large military transport in two days' time, from where they would fly to the smaller Vigie Airport in St. Lucia aboard smaller aircraft.

Frank asked Terry and me to organize a party for the VIPs. A special plane was coming from Texas, he explained, with two hundred pounds of premium steak and fresh produce. Leroy's empty oil drum band was to be on standby and we were asked to invite the entire St. Lucia government, as well as the British representatives, Lord and Lady Oxford. Frank wanted all the prominent people on the island there to meet the U.S. brass.

Terry and I went into emergency operations mode as "D-Day" approached. The hotel was spiffed and cleaned and Joel, whom I had recently put in command of the *Ramona*, was put on standby. On the appointed day, the first of the military planes landed in Martinique and, later that day, the wives of the various officials began to arrive in Marigot Bay. Frank owned a Beechcraft Bonanza aircraft, which he sent down to help ferry them from Martinique to Vigie Airport. Apparently, the wives had been sent on ahead, as the husbands were delayed due to some important affairs of state.

The wives had no idea of what to expect. They were enthralled by the beauty of Marigot Bay and enjoyed themselves tremendously the first evening, sipping our bartender Hypolyte's banana daiquiris, while chatting to each other by the bar. Even Leroy's steel band was a hit.

By the next morning, the wives were settled in, but none of the husbands had appeared. The military men were held up, I was informed, by developments in the Far East, but they would be coming soon. Meanwhile, the wives were getting restless and looking for something to do. There were lots of questions like, "Where is the golf course?" or "Where are the tennis courts?" and "Where would I find the beauty parlor?" Unfortunately, we were unable to supply any such amenities, and so the wives stayed at the bar and Hypolyte continued to dispense his daiquiris.

Another day passed and by the next morning, Terry and I were worried. The big party was scheduled for that evening, but there were no husbands around and the wives were demanding to know what was going on. I called Frank.

"Frank, when are these people of yours arriving? I've got Lord and Lady Oxford arriving tonight, along with half the island and there's a group of rather angry women here, I told him. "You better get those men down here fast."

"Don't worry Walter, I think we may have everything settled here:' Frank assured me, "and general this and admiral that will arrive tomorrow afternoon with senator so and so."

"But Frank, the party is tonight. Lord and Lady Oxford are going to be highly offended if you and the others aren't here. The whole St. Lucia government is going to be here with fifty of the island's most important people. What do you want me to do?"

"You're going to have to postpone it for a few days." Frank said, and that was that. Terry and I went through the embarrassment of cancelling the soiree. Telling the politicians was bad enough, but the frost came on the windows at government house when Lord and Lady Oxford were informed. The following day I called Frank again.

"Frank, you'd better get some husbands down here because there's talk of divorce going on."

"No can do, Walter, another problem has arisen." Frank replied apologetically, "Maybe you can send them on a short cruise. The men aren't going to be finished for a few more days."

The ladies were delighted with the idea, and they were shifted aboard the *Ramona*, which was ready to sail under Joel's command. I told them they were going for a cruise of the Grenadines, a beautiful area to the south of St. Lucia. So, with young Joel at the helm, the schooner sailed out of Marigot Bay with a cargo of congressmen's and admirals' wives aboard, and a crew of ten. It was wintertime and the trade winds were blowing strong from the north-northeast. As soon as the *Ramona* spread her wings, she disappeared quickly over the horizon, lee rail down.

As luck would have it, no sooner had her sails disappeared, the phone began ringing. It was Frank calling to say that everything was cleared up and the men would begin arriving tomorrow.

The whole fiasco started up again. Frank and his entourage of generals, admirals, senators, and congressmen arrived, and loved the bay. Hypolyte couldn't fill the glasses fast enough and the cardboard box he kept to throw empty booze bottles in was soon filled to the brim. The first night was a roaring success. They all joked about how great it was for them to be sitting at the bar, while their wives were off sailing on a schooner. The seemingly humorous aspect of this situation was, however, short lived.

The following morning, everyone congregated on the hotel terrace and Admiral Carney cross-examined me.

"Walter, let me see if I have this right. You've sent the *Ramona* down to the Grenadines with our wives, and she's a schooner capable of more than twelve knots." I nodded for him to continue. "Now, my pilot has a yacht of his own and he tells me that the *Ramona* could be back tomorrow if we radio them now. Would you please oblige?"

I knew I was in trouble now. Facing the military might of the United States I said, "Admiral Carney, I don't know where the *Ramona* is right now, nor can I contact her as we don't have ship-to-shore telephone here, and as far as coming back at twelve knots, well the wind is very contrary at the moment, and it would be a slow and rough return trip at best."

I could see this news wasn't sitting too well with these admirals and politicians, and I swallowed as they quietly digested my words. The next man to speak was Mendel Rivers, a big man with long white hair and bushy eyebrows. "Captain Boudreau, are you telling us that you've sent our wives off to some little islands, you're not sure where they are at the moment, and you have no way of contacting them to get them back?"

I straightened my back and replied, "That is the situation, sir."

There was a bit of turmoil amongst the ranks then and the big shots quickly turned on Frank.

"Well Frank, what the hell are you going to do?" they said. "You got us into all this."

OPERATION RUM BOTTLE

There was silence. Frank and I could do nothing, save to sit and rack our brains for a way to resolve the situation. Even the kids were fascinated by this scene and were perched on the edge of their chairs watching and waiting.

"I know what to do." a familiar voice suddenly chirped up and all eyes turned towards the speaker. It was Terry. With a slight bow and a sweeping gesture of the hand, Mendel Rivers turned to my wife.

"Ma'am, you have the floor;" he offered in a deep voice.

Terry stood up in her flowered dress, and as if this were an everyday affair, addressed the masters of the U.S. military.

"Well," she said smiling, "If you can't telephone them, why doesn't Walter fly down with the pilot of one of your fast airplanes and tell Joel to come back?"

"But ma'am, how can he tell Joel if he can't radio from the plane?" one of the generals asked.

Unfazed, my ever-resourceful wife answered quickly. "That's easy. Just fill up a dozen or so of the empty rum bottles with notes and Walter can throw them out of the window when they find the *Ramona*."

There was another silence, followed by a few murmurs amongst our red-eyed top brass. Mendel Rivers lightened the tone by pointing out that after last night there would be no shortage of empty booze bottles. At that moment, I thought that any plan was a good one, and everyone else seemed impressed by Terry's idea. "Operation Rum Bottle" was activated immediately. I was never prouder of my wife.

The next morning, Terry drove me to Vigie Airport, and I climbed into the twin-engine plane next to the pilot. She passed up the cardboard box full of rum bottles, all of which contained the same message; "Captain Joel, sailing yacht *Ramona*. Come home now, the men are in Marigot." Attached to each bottle was a long-colored streamer.

The pilot and I took off and flew quickly south. It was a fast plane, and we were soon making a circuit of the Grenadines. Passing over the island of Bequia, I spotted *Ramona*'s tall masts.

"There she is." I said to the pilot, and we got ready to drop our bombs.

"Just be careful not to hit the stabilizers when you throw the bottles out." he shouted to me.

I had always been wary of small aircraft and his warning left me feeling a little uncomfortable. I opened a window in the side of the cockpit and as we divebombed Bequia Harbor, I carefully threw out all the liquor bottles. We could see the local boys rowing out in their boats collecting the bottles.

We found out later that not only did Joel get the message many times over, but the cheeky boys also asked him to pay, charging anywhere from one to three of the local "Bee Wee" dollars per bottle. He stopped paying once he found out that all the bottles contained the same message.

Joel got underway soon afterwards and made the uncomfortable slog to windward under reduced canvas. It was squally and rough, with gusts to forty knots or more, but the schooner arrived the next morning and the wives were glad to get ashore. Some headed straight for their husbands to give them a kiss, while others headed straight to Hypolyte for one of his daiquiris.

The following evening, Frank Jameson finally had his party and even Lord and Lady Oxford managed the long drive to Marigot. Leroy and his empty oil drum band pinged away, and the drinks flowed freely.

Rivers slept on the anchored *Ramona* for the balance of his visit and would drink a glass or two of rum while watching the sun set from the stern. Lou, Peter, Janeen, and little Brian sat and talked with him for a while one evening. They told him about the fish, the sea, and of the local characters who lived on the island. As they sat on the deck at his feet, he looked at my children from under those great bushy eyebrows of his and listened intently. Who knows what he saw in the eyes of these half wild young kids in the southern islands? Perhaps a trusting innocence, gone forever from his own way of life.

Later, during the winter of 1965, Admiral Carney chartered the *Ramona* for a two-week cruise from Barbados to St. Croix. He came with his wife and six guests. I was in command at the time and Lou, Peter, and Janeen were at boarding school in Barbados. In fact, the three of them had just sailed up from St. Lucia with me and I deposited them at their respective schools before going to the airport to meet Admiral Carney.

We left Barbados at dusk with the intention of running down to St. Lucia, visiting the ports there and then proceeding north along the island chain, ending up at St. Croix in the U.S. Virgin Islands. I was wondering whether I would run into any problems with my guest, especially considering he was the first admiral with which I had ever sailed.

Unfortunately, things didn't get off to a very good start. As soon as we left the lee of Barbados, the *Ramona* sunk her shoulder into the sizeable trade wind waves, running off at well over twelve knots. There was a good stiff breeze, and the schooner was doing what she had been built to do. Admiral Carney came to me after dinner and told me he would be retiring now and could he open the porthole over his bunk in the cabin, as he was finding it a touch stuffy. He was on the port side, which was the low side, and the *Ramona* was blazing along with her portholes mostly out of the water, but once in a while she would take a deep roll and put her midship ports under green water. The admiral was in the aft cabin however, and I told him it would probably be alright, but that he should keep an eye out and close the porthole before he went to sleep.

Mrs. Carney was a very down to earth person, who didn't say anything unless it was worthwhile and I probably should have caught her eye when the admiral started looking for little favors. Anyway, just before midnight the wettest admiral you ever saw came up in his pajamas.

"Do you have any idea what has happened?" he asked me in an angry tone.

I did in fact have a pretty good idea of what had happened, judging from his soggy pajamas. But, before I could think of a reply he continued.

"Captain, my mattress is soaking, I am soaking. Why did you tell me to open the porthole?"

Since I was running my own vessel and not answerable to anyone, I was considering how to subdue the angry admiral, when Mrs. Carney came up the companionway dry as a bone and gave her husband a dirty look.

"Robert, you're a goddamn admiral, and if you don't have enough brains to close your own porthole, you can't blame it on the captain." she admonished.

We placated him by providing him with another mattress and clean dry sheets. I also had the steward close the porthole, of course.

Admiral Carney and I became good friends over the coming days. We would often sit in the doghouse late into the night drinking coffee, laced with a drop or two of rum, and talk about the war. We remained in touch over the years.

LANDFALL AT AVES, - ISLE OF BIRDS

Nothing is quite as magical as a Caribbean sunrise at sea. As morning broke, the waves came alive with new color, changing from the leaden grey of night to a sparkling rich West Indian blue, capped by pristine white crests. The salt spray was clean and salty and as it jumped over the rail into my face, I felt invigorated and refreshed.

We were on a voyage to the mysterious lost atoll of the Caribbean with the schooner *Ramona*. We were on a charter with one passenger who had an insatiable interest in this legend. Aves lay in the middle of the Caribbean Sea, a spot of sand and coral known mostly as a legend that few men had ever seen.

The great Northeast Trade Winds always eased somewhat during the night, but in the first hour or so of daylight, they usually increased. Puffy white clouds scudded along ever westward beneath the crisp blue sky and the day seemed fresh and new. Indeed, new adventures and excitement lay before us that I could not have imagined.

The schooner *Ramona* awoke to the bustle of another day under sail. The captain called everyone at dawn and all hands were on deck. Usually, the first chore was to reset the deep-sea trolling lines.

"Don't set those this morning." he told us, "With any luck at all we'll be making landfall at Aves very soon."

Wilfred was on lookout duty, but we all had our eyes peeled expectantly. Because of its remoteness, low profile and small size, many capable seafarers had been unable to find Aves. Our destination had justifiably earned its nickname, The Lost Atoll.

Aves appeared suddenly before us as if by magic. First, there were only white crested waves on a blue Caribbean, but a moment later a desolate spit of white sand and sun-bleached coral rose out of the sea. I could not have imagined such a place.

"Land off de starboard bow skip." Wilfred called from where he was standing lookout near the foremast.

Running forward to see for myself, I peered off in the direction Wilfred had pointed over the bow of the schooner, and I saw Aves for the first time. This was truly a paradoxical place, surviving where it should not be able to survive. About a quarter mile long by five hundred feet wide the sandy atoll sat on a circular volcanic tooth that had been colonized be tiny coral polyps and formed the traditional ring of reef and inner lagoon. Over time the lip of the ancient volcanic crater, eroded away leaving only a small, curved section that was the present-day Aves. The islet was continuously eroded and rebuilt.

Over the centuries, vicious storms vented their fury on the tiny islet and Aves would be washed away only to be rebuilt again. Mostly sand and bits of bleached out dry coral, it was partially surrounded by a coral reef that acted as a rampart, no doubt saving it from totally disappearing over the centuries. The water was clear and clean and shallow soundings went out a hundred yards or so from the shoreline before plummeting into the deep.

White surf broke on the windward side of the atoll where the Caribbean spent itself on protecting the sand and coral bulwark. Plumes of spray rode the wind over Aves' sandy midriff to fall on the lee side in occasional whiffs of salty mist. There was no real harbor, but the west and leeward side offered a fair if not good anchorage in calm weather.

As the *Ramona's* bowsprit traced a slow rise and fall against the horizon, we prepared to make our landfall.

"Lower away from forward." the skipper called, and he momentarily ran the schooner off for the headsails to come down before rounding her bows to the wind.

We struck canvas quickly and as we stowed sail the schooner's motions decreased until she was moving only slightly. Finally, her bow turned towards the shore, and we made our way slowly into shallower water.

"Stand by to take soundings." the skipper called, and I made ready with the lead line.

This was the traditional mariner's depth measuring device comprising a long line with a large tubular lead weight at the end. It was marked with colored bits of rag and leather thongs indicating fathoms or units of six feet. Standing with my back braced against the starboard lower foremast shrouds and one foot on the heavy teak caprail, I coiled the line carefully on the deck and prepared to cast as far forward as I could using my right hand.

"Soundings," the skipper called a moment later and I began swinging the line.

Heaving the lead forward it splashed some thirty feet ahead of the schooner. Allowing the knots and markers to run through my hand I watched to see which one stopped closest to the surface of the water when the lead hit bottom.

"By the mark six," I called over my shoulder.

"By the mark six."

"By the mark and a half five."

"By the mark five."

Then the schooner came over the sandy bank of the lagoon and the bottom shoaled sharply.

"By the mark three," I called, and the skipper responded quickly.

"Stop sounding and stand by the anchor." he shouted forward.

Wilfred and Philius swung the big three-hundred-pound fisherman anchor out on the davit. Philius stood with the quick release lanyard to the gallows hook in his hand. When the bow of the schooner was in about eighteen feet of water, the skipper decided it was close enough.

"Let go," he called.

"Let go," the mate repeated as he yanked the lanyard.

The big anchor hit the water with a splash and sank to the sandy bottom. The inch and a half stud link chain rattled out behind it leaving the smell of rust and a little cloud of reddish powder that blew downwind over the schooner's deck.

Ahead of us on the thin strip of white sand, what seemed like thousands of sea birds suddenly took flight, screeching and wheeling overhead. Although there must have been other species, I immediately saw brown boobies, pristine white tropicbirds, black frigates with red chests, and some white terns as well.

The swift sleek boobies stayed low, skimming the surface of the sea on wide wings before diving suddenly to catch a meal. They dove beneath the surface after their prey and must have been good swimmers. You could see their slender wings fold behind them a split second before they hit the water.

The frigates were huge birds with wingspans over six feet and although I had seen many before I had never seen so many together at one time. Ciseaux is the French name for them and justly so. The long twin tail feathers that they used as ailerons opened and closed as they flew like a pair of giant scissors. There must have been hundreds. They wheeled high above the other birds seemingly aloof, waiting for a larger sized fish to swim near the surface. Plummeting like Kamikaze pilots, they deftly plucked their prey with long beaks. They were able to pull out of their dives at the last possible moment and I never saw one crash into the sea.

The snow-white tropicbirds had long tails and shorter wings that beat fast all the time. They flitted about in the shallows near the surface picking up little fish and any bits dropped by the larger birds. In later years, I would see these small ocean wanderers hundreds of miles from land.

Aves provided a stopover for migrating birds traveling from North America to the huge marshes of northern Venezuela. I saw many other species of birds at Aves that I could not identify other than the fact that they were not sea birds, just weary flyers that had stopped to have a rest before going on.

The birds screeched and squawked wheeling above the schooner. They seemed upset by our intrusion, by our brazenness at daring to enter their timeless refuge.

I felt a sense of awe at our presence there, one of earth's strangest locations to be sure.

THE CALL OF THE SEA
Mishap on the Bluenose II

At the age of seventeen I joined the schooner *Bluenose II* as a deckhand when she was at the island of St. Lucia in the West Indies. My father was a good friend of Captain Ellsworth Coggins, master of this famous Canadian sailing ship. In the early sixties, the Oland family of Nova Scotia built a replica of the famed schooner at the same Lunenburg shipyard that had built the first, calling her Bluenose II. She visited our home in Marigot Bay, St Lucia many times in those years. We would watch her long black hull come slowly into the inner harbor and drop her hook to windward before putting stern lines to the coconut trees on the sand spit.

My father was running his fleet of big schooners out of Marigot Bay. He had spoken to Captain Coggins several times on my behalf and my name was put forward in the hopes that I might get a job. Part of the agreement I had with my parents about not returning to school was that I would go to sea on ships other than my father's. They felt that it would be best if I left the bay and got a bit of experience on other vessels. I loved the islands but agreed that I should get out and be my own man.

And so, I managed to get aboard the *Bluenose II*. I was lucky; indeed, there was a long waiting list of young Canadian lads ready to sail on her. It was only circumstance and my father's help that secured the job. So, I signed on the ship's articles as an ordinary seaman. After signing the book in the chartroom with Captain Coggins, I went on deck where I asked a seaman named Dave Rawding what O.D. stood for.

"Ordinary Seaman, mush for brains," he replied with a grin.

Our engineer was one Rodney Himmelman from Lunenburg, and the mate was a fine Norwegian seaman named Oddmund Skodje. Bosun Neil Dalkier was another good man from Denmark. There were another half dozen men. I soon settled into the routine of the schooner, and I found that I was able to hold my own and perform my duties to the mate's satisfaction even though I was just seventeen. My prior experience had laid a good foundation for this moment in my life, and I was happy. The *Bluenose II* was a fine schooner, and the crew was a good bunch as well.

We carried out charter cruises in the Caribbean Islands including the Leeward and Virgin Islands, and the big schooner ate up the strong Trade Winds. The open channels between the islands offered good stiff breezes for the big schooner and I was thrilled when it was my turn at the helm. It was quite an experience for a young lad to feel this powerful vessel with her four-thousand square foot mainsail and eighty-four-foot main boom heel over and reap the wind. She would settle her round bilge into the blue Caribbean and really move. At twelve knots she seemed to be making no effort at all. Initially the mate watched me carefully at the helm, but the *Bluenose II* steered easily and before long I had taken her measure. From then on, the mate and skipper left me alone in the confidence that I would keep her on course.

The Oland family came for a few weeks, and we sailed them to the Tobago Cays where I took them out to World's End Reef to snorkel. I took the small whaler out early in the morning and speared a dozen or so lobsters for the owners.

I soon discovered that there was a wonderful cargo stowed in the hold of the *Bluenose II*. Hundreds of cases of "Schooner Beer." The owners of the ship, Oland Brewery, built her as a promotional tool, and she was a great success. On the side of every can there was the saying "You can't beat a good schooner." which referred to the original *Bluenose's* unbeaten winning streak. There was no drinking age in the fo'c'sle of this schooner and I soon developed a taste for that lovely golden brew.

All too soon the charter season ended in the islands, and we headed for Nova Scotia. This was home for most of the crew and they were all looking forward to being reunited with their families after so many months away.

After a stop in Bermuda, we arrived in Halifax to a fine welcome. The families and friends of the crew were all there to meet them and it was a grand reunion. Soon though there were only a few of us left on the ship and we stood watch while the others enjoyed a hard-earned rest.

UNDER THE TRADE WIND SKY

A few weeks after our arrival in Nova Scotia the captain passed down the word that we would be doing some day trips with passengers out of Halifax harbor. We were given new uniforms with baggy navy style trousers and tops with *Bluenose II* on the front. My trousers were a little big and the cuffs were very loose around my shoes.

Soon the vessel's decks were crammed with day-trippers, and we were all enjoying this new kind of sailing. Each morning we would set all sails and drift on out past McNabs Island into the open water toward Chebucto Head before tacking to sail back into the harbor.

During those warm summer days sailing in Halifax harbor, we young lads were intrigued by another thing as well, the number of young, single women who came out for a sail. Young fellows being young fellows we were inclined to show off a bit and generally make fools of ourselves. I took the cake in that respect.

During one of our day sails out of the harbor I noticed a very pretty young blond girl, probably my own age, and she seemed to express a great deal of interest in my work on the deck. I just carried on and smiled at her when I could in the expectation that I would get the courage to talk to her after the sail.

As we approached our berth in the harbor the mate ordered us to lower away sail and I decided to make a show of my job. Lowering the huge mainsail required care. The two large rope halyards were eased over the heavy belaying pins at the main mast tabernacle into big wooden pulley blocks on the deck.

Instead of paying attention to what I was doing I kept on looking back over my shoulder at the blond girl and smiling at her. Suddenly I felt something tugging at my leg. While not paying attention to my task, the cuff of my trousers had been sucked into the big pulley block. I looked down in dismay as my pants slid down my waist. The young blond girl sensed that something was amiss and had stopped smiling at me. She was now covering her mouth with her hand and giggling.

Lowering away had to be carried out in unison. The throat halyard and the peak had to be kept going at more or less equal speed. But to save my dignity I stopped lowering in the sail. Skodje the mate caught it right away.

"Hey! Lower away!" he shouted at me.

Glancing over I could see him scowling. I was in a predicament. I had to lower away but I was in danger of totally losing my pants. I slacked another foot or so over the pin but as the heavy manila rope inexorably pulled the cloth of my pants through the pulley the rear seam of my trouser began to tear, and to my total horror the trousers slipped over my rear end and down. Then my leg was pulled up to the block and I could go no further.

Skodje appeared fuming, but as soon as he saw me, he grinned.

"Showing off for the girls, eh?" he asked whipping out his knife.

As the mate cut away the remnants of my trousers, so the final remnants of my dignity vanished as well.

Yup, mortally embarrassed.

There was also a lot of giggling going on and I dared to look behind me. The blond girl was giggling along with her friends.

"Lower away, what are you waiting for now?" Skodje asked loudly.

I turned to the belaying pin and began to ease the big manila rope over the tabernacle rail. I remembered that the underwear I was wearing had a hole in the seat. So, with one side of my navy pants gone, the other in tatters and my pride crushed we lowered the sail and as soon as we had made fast the halyards Skodje nodded for me to go below. I ran forward to the fo'c'sle hatch went below and quickly changed. With new trousers I returned to the deck to help handle the dock lines and help disembark the passengers.

In kindness the blond girl stepped aside at the gangway to speak to me for moment.

"Don't worry," she said, "It was funny, but it could have happened to anyone."

"Thanks" I said, still humiliated. Marshalling all my courage I looked at her blue eyes.

"Do you, live here?"

"No, I'm from Ontario," she replied smiling, "but thanks for a nice trip."

I said goodbye and she walked up the gangway to the dock. I felt better but she was only a tourist and I never saw her again.

My shipmates lost no time in making my humiliation the butt of their jokes and for a few days I suffered their ribbing, but I never again took my eyes off the main halyard blocks.

Brave men rescue the crew of the SC 709.

A True Canadian Hero

Every once in a while, history presents us with an individual who can only be described as a hero. My siblings and I were certainly blessed to have a father whose actions during the World War II can only be described as such.

It was December 1943 and my father, merchant seaman Walter Boudreau, joined the barquentine *Angelus* loading lumber in Louisbourg, Nova Scotia bound for the West Indies. She was a large square-rigged windjammer of 238 tons. At that time, the *SC709*, a 120-foot U.S. naval vessel was bound from Norfolk, Virginia to St. John's, Newfoundland for anti-submarine patrol service. Coming up the Nova Scotia coast, in a full gale, ice began to form on the vessel's superstructure. They tried to shelter in Louisbourg, but she struck the reef outside Louisbourg harbor. Soon the freezing seas made her look more like an iceberg than a ship.

Everyone in Louisbourg, soon learned of the *SC709*. The crew of the U.S. vessel pleaded desperately over the radio with the shore station to send help quickly, but there seemed to be little anyone could do to help. Louisbourg was a small fishing town, with no Coast Guard or rescue facilities of any kind and few of the fishermen were in commission.

Captain Jensen of the *Angelus* was a man of action and realized that if something was not done soon, the U.S. sailors would perish. He called for some volunteers from the crew and every man stood forward.

The mate, Art Holmans, and my father agreed to row together, and the *Angelus* crew swung two dories into horse-drawn carts on the dock and carried them to the shore opposite the wreck where they dragged the dories to the water's edge.

Art and my father floated their dory and began pulling against the wind and the freezing sea. Their woolen mitts were soon wet and frozen to the oars. Each gust of wind brought a hail of freezing spray, stinging their faces like attacking wasps.

Reaching the wreck, they banged on the hull with their oars. The *SC709* resembled a huge block of ice. Finally, one of the pilot house windows burst outwards and some heads appeared. They were extremely glad to see the dory men. My father and Art helped two U.S. sailors over the rail and settling them in the bottom of the dory pulled their stern line for the shore. Later a lobster boat came to help as well. All twenty-six crew members of the *USS SC709* were saved that day.

Following the *SC709* rescue, the *Angelus* crew prepared for the voyage south with their cargo of lumber for Barbados. On March 5th, the barquentine made an offing for the West Indies. It was cold tough work. The ropes were difficult to make fast or coil and the seaman's hands were numb.

The *Angelus* laid a course of due south and by mid-afternoon, they were sailing well. Soon they left behind the grey-green seas of the north Atlantic and crossed into the deep blue waters of the Gulf Stream. They made port in Barbados a few weeks later and after unloading their lumber they set sail for Nova Scotia.

On May 19th, the *Angelus* was approximately four hundred miles off the U.S. coast. The sun rose as usual, but this particular morning brought along with it the horror of war. There was a sinister-looking black-hulled submarine on the surface not three hundred yards distant, making its way towards them.

After a warning shot from the submarine's deck cannon, the *Angelus* launched the lifeboat and the crew, along with Captain Jensen and his little dog Mutty, got into it and rowed away from the *Angelus*.

The captain of the submarine signaled for them to come over and they rowed to within forty feet of the menacing long black hull. They stopped alongside the submarine and hoisted their hands in the air. The submarine commander gave them a few minutes to row away from the *Angelus* and then they sank her with their foredeck gun.

They were somewhere north of Bermuda and south-southeast of George's Bank. The lifeboat was poorly equipped. There were only the four bent oars, and in any case, there was no hope of rowing the hundreds of miles to shore. The weather was cold, and the sun never showed itself from behind an overcast sky. At the end of the second day, they began to experience some swells. That night the lifeboat capsized. There were some scattered replies and my father saw the shadowy forms of others, but Captain Jensen and his little dog were gone.

Righting the boat they sat on the thwarts through the darkness, waist deep in the icy water. The mate's son died the next day while his father Art held him closely in his arms. He was trying to keep his son warm, but it was too late. My father took Sandy from him, letting him over the side and he joined the others who had gone into the deep. This was the morning of their tenth day adrift in the north Atlantic. The mate Art Holman and my father were they last ones left.

Then there were voices and the blurry vision of a grey ship's side and netting near them. A U.S. destroyer escort had found them, and they were saved. They were grateful, but for Art it was a bitter salvation. He left part of his soul somewhere to the southeast of George's Bank with his son.

This tale is dedicated to all those gallant men and women who served in the merchant marine during World War II. Some came back but many did not.

Let us take a moment today to remember them.

Shere Khan in Civitavecchia, Italy prior to our voyage west.

Fire at Sea

"**M**ayday, Mayday, Mayday, we have a fire aboard." the chilling radio transmission that we all hope never to make. The thought of a fire aboard far from land is a sobering one, but it's a scenario that can and does occur. Many sailors take their little ships into the Great Atlantic to voyage to warmer climes during the winter. It is to them that I humbly offer a few words of wisdom. Those of us who take small ships into the great ocean need to be cognizant of this latent danger and take precautions in advance. One of the best tools in this respect is prior awareness. Recognizing fire as a possible hazard puts you way ahead of the game.

It goes without saying that a fire at sea is more potentially dangerous than it would be ashore. There are no fire departments out there and you can't escape to the lawn outside your home to watch the blaze. You're stuck in situation and unless there's a nearby port with coast guard facilities you'll be dealing with the problem yourself. A number of yachts are visited by this blight every year resulting in millions of dollars' worth of damage but more importantly though, the threat of personal injury or death always lurks.

Fires occur on cruise ships, warships, all manner of commercial vessels, and of course on yachts. Caused when certain circumstances combine to promote combustion, two of the top culprits of yacht fires are galley fat and propane but other candidates include potentially dangerous materials such as outboard gasoline, paint thinners, and our stern BBQ. Increasingly however, we find another gremlin raising its head. While shipboard fires have occurred throughout history, today's modern yacht or powerboat is a far cry from those of 30 or even 10 years ago. She will be a far more sophisticated machine with numerous intricate systems requiring dedicated maintenance. If the vessel was designed for long range cruising, her systems will be duplicated in many cases providing offshore security and reliability. Inevitably, the very complexity of the systems often ends up being the root cause of many problems. As anyone who has had anything to do with yachts will confirm, salt water and electrical circuitry do not make good bedfellows, and most modern yachts have their share. Sometimes all it takes is a little water on a junction box to set off a spark. After that, all bets are off.

If you're planning an offshore voyage or even a short coastal trip you should look at this situation carefully. While there are no black and white blueprints that apply to each specific situation, statistics show that most fires are preventable and there are several clearly beneficial ideas pertaining to the causes, prevention, and cure for fires afloat. For starters, your marine safety regulations provide rules that insure a good first line of defense. You can go further though, and our own experience is a good case in point. We'll go back to when my wife and I along with a crew of six were taking a 100-foot ketch from the eastern Mediterranean to the West Indies.

We departed bound for the West Indies via Gibraltar and the Canary Islands. The 150-ton yacht appeared to be a well-found vessel in excellent condition and with all required safety equipment. An automatic engine room/fuel alleyway fire system protected the machinery spaces while individual fire extinguishers of the required size and type were situated in every compartment as well as on deck and in the lazarette. With a total of six experienced crew aboard we sailed westbound through the Strait of Bonifacio.

The voyage proceeded without incident until we ran into some bad weather just east-northeast of the Canary Islands. With strong head winds from the southwest gusting to 50 knots at times, the powerful steel sailing yacht was handling it surprisingly well. Flying a 40 percent reefed main and staysail to hold her steady we kept the big 400 hp main engine at about ¼ throttle to help keep her head into it. With the inhospitable African coast a few hundred miles to leeward we were well-motivated towards keeping her going in the right direction however slowly. A heavy and very confused sea ran every which way and although her high bows rose to meet each challenge she was taking considerable water on deck from time to time.

Around 2:00 p.m. in the afternoon all hell suddenly broke loose. My wife and I were off watch and resting in the aft cabin when we caught the unmistakable smell of electrical shorting. A few moments later wafts of smoke began coming through the air-conditioning ducts.

Within a matter of seconds, the smoke thickened and by the time we rushed out the door black acrid clouds had filled the aft cabin.

Calling all hands on deck we immediately sheeted in flat and put the vessel's bow as close as possible into the wind without luffing. From the cockpit we noticed black smoke issuing from around the teak lazarette hatch rim and I rushed aft to investigate. Even though it was wet the stern deck was warm beneath my feet. We attempted to open the hatch using the hydraulic toggle switch, but it had already been rendered inoperative; the hatch was being held shut by the locked hydraulic ram.

Reducing engine rpms to steerageway only, the mate and I rushed to the engine room. This compartment held smoke as well, but we managed to switch off the a/c system and electrical power to the aft section of the vessel before returning to the master cabin. Breaking off the air screens we emptied two extinguishers into the ducting vents.

Back on deck we looked helplessly at the lazarette. The five feet square teak and aluminum hatch was controlled by a hydraulic ram system that was now rendered inoperative by the fire within. With dismay we realized that we faced the nasty situation of having a fire inside with no access to it except through this heavy hatch which was now seized shut! And there was no manual override in the system.

With crowbars and big screwdrivers, the mate and I fought to open the hatch working against 500 pounds of locked down hydraulic pressure. Looking back, I realize that we accomplished something that we normally would not have been able to do. Fear is a great motivator and the fact that we were desperate probably gave us that something extra to get it open, but we finally managed. Lashing it open we looked down inside and another chill ran down my spine. There was little time left. The compartment contained the ships designated paint locker. There were cans of varnish, thinners, plus other possibly flammable gear in the bulkhead lockers. Flames flickered behind the bulkhead and smoke billowed out. I knew that we were at a critical point – if the fire got any worse it might become uncontrollable with disastrous results. We had to try and put it out as quickly as possible.

Kneeling at the edge I emptied the large cockpit fire extinguisher at the smoking bulkhead before jumping down into the compartment. Opening the doors to the paint shelves I emptied the big pilothouse fire canister there before starting to toss cans up to the mate, who in turn quickly tossed them over the side. With a wet tea towel over my nose and mouth I kept passing stuff up. Some of the cans were quite hot. We quickly jettisoned anything possibly flammable over the side. After twenty minutes or so the fire was out.

At the beginning of the emergency, I had asked one of the delivery crew, a qualified captain himself to radio out our situation but the antenna couplers were situated in the lazarette and had been damaged. After numerous attempts he couldn't raise anyone on either the SSB or VHF and I told him to activate the two EPIRBS we had on board. The signals went out and a helicopter was on the scene approximately five hours after receiving the signal.

Approximately two hours after the fire started we were confident that it was completely out. Repetitive checks indicated there was no longer any evidence of smoke inside the vessel and so we put her on a course for Puerto Rosario on the island of Fuerteventura. The weather had abated somewhat by this time, and we made port several hours later. After tying up alongside a fishing trawler we carefully examined the site of the fire. Apparently salt water from the waves coming over the aft deck had been making its way into the lazarette where it began shorting the ample electrical circuitry there.

There were some injuries to the crew, but we survived this dangerous situation. It also left us with some pretty clear conclusions. I've listed them below. I firmly believe that they all have a bearing on where we are today.

All ship's fire equipment was reviewed and brought up to date before we left Italy. The expiration dates on all fire extinguishers were carefully checked and those that had expired were replaced or refilled. When we urgently needed them they worked. Make sure your fire equipment is up to date and in good working order.

1. Our life rafts, flares, etc., were serviced and checked as well. Even though we never got to the abandon ship stage I was secure in the knowledge that if needed they would be available. Be sure that all your safety equipment is current and in good nick before you leave port. A cavalier attitude in this respect could someday cost you your life.

2. I believe that we were able to beat this fire mainly because we managed to get it under control early before it flared uncontrollably. The jettisoning of flammable materials

prevented a marginal fire from becoming a raging uncontrollable inferno. Although every emergency will be slightly different the fact that we chose various courses of action and moved quickly paid off. Act in a timely fashion.

3. The sleeping arrangements I had assigned for the delivery to the West Indies were such that there was a crewmember in every compartment of the boat. It was specifically set out this way so that if there were a problem in any cabin the crew would become aware of it sooner. This certainly paid off in our case. If you are a hired skipper you may want to recount this to your owner and his wife…they'll encourage you to sleep in their aft cabin.

4. The fire was electrical in origin. By shutting down power to the affected sections of the ship, it prevented further shorting of electrical systems. I believe that this may have prevented the fire spreading. Thoroughly familiarize yourself with the ship's systems before you leave port.

5. A vigilant crew was not caught off guard. Through keeping traditional sea watches, we were able to detect, fight, and bring under control a situation that could have developed into a disaster. Before leaving Italy we made sure that everyone was thoroughly familiar with all on board safety equipment, its location and use. Early on in the voyage we conducted a man overboard and lifeboat drill.

Putting the ship's head into the wind is a recognized tactic if a fire occurs in the aft section of the vessel. It prevented smoke and flames from blowing back onto the vessel and possibly compounding an already dangerous situation.

Stow all dangerous materials carefully. Instruct your guests as to the location of your outboard gas jerry can and where you keep it on deck. If you allow smoking aboard make sure there is a spark free zone surrounding the gas stowage area. Know exactly where your flammables are kept and monitor them carefully.

Carefully check your propane connections with soap and water and make sure you gas cylinders are located at a legal non-vapor-holding site.

Safe sailing doesn't just happen, we make it so. Spending that extra day going over your safety systems while still at the dock could make all the difference. Certainly, you'll feel just that much more secure in the knowledge that your vessel is ready for whatever comes along. Some might say we were lucky but I believe that it was our attitude along with some careful preparation and vigilance that left us where we are today; alive.

Could we have done it better, or different, to improve the outcome? I've thought about this a lot over the years, but I can't honestly think of anything I would have really done much differently. I can think of a number of other experiences where I certainly might have done things a lot differently but this was probably one of those few times where we got it all just right!! I think the fact that all of the crew survived and that the ship is still sailing speaks to that. In fact, I believe a potential tragedy was averted by the means mentioned above.

If there were a couple of small things that I would add they would be these.

6. Have at least one or more, larger portable fire extinguishers located centrally. I know a big fire extinguisher is hard to stow and awkward to handle but if you really needed it, it would be worth its weight in diamonds. The ones aboard were fully charged, inspected, and of the recommended size and type, but one really big one would have come in handy.

7. The vessel probably could have benefitted from a slightly higher capacity engine room exhaust fan system. The one on board was certainly adequate and did the job, but a slightly bigger one would have helped clear the air a few moments sooner.

8. When I think back to how close we came to actually getting the life rafts out I think I will always keep a couple of jerry cans with "ready" fresh water on deck. Although life rafts do have a certain amount of water there is never enough. I would keep them only two thirds full so that they would float of their own accord. This is a well-known precaution that many ocean cruising sailors take in case they are ever required to "get off" in mid ocean. I certainly support the idea; you can't have too much water!

FIRE AT SEA

Whatever the size and type of your vessel you will be required to carry appropriate fire/safety equipment on board. All seafarers should check that they have the required equipment on board and that it is not expired and shipshape. There's no rule saying you can't increase your fire-fighting inventory to standards beyond those required by law. I always do. Remember, awareness and care are your best friends at sea. Safe sailing!

A Sea of Dreams

And so the years have passed like leaves on the wind and my life has been like a magical dream. I was blessed with a wonderful memory, and I would share my thoughts as I recall the wonders of the world, I want to share these with any who would hear them.

I was born a child of the sea and in my mind the pictures of those years are clear and beautiful. The stars in the night sky above the sails of the tall ship running before the wind were a wonder to behold. The dawn would break and bring to life a beautiful blue ocean, and my innocent gaze over the windward rail brought the salt spray to my face.

As a child under sail, I saw the coastlines of many countries beginning in the place of my birth where the regal green pine trees rose from sandy shores to lovely, forested hills.

My voyages took me to see the deserts of north Africa and the ancient coastal towns and villages of the historic Mediterranean Sea. I have felt the heat of the burning Sirocco in my face and rode a camel into the Al-Rif mountains to gaze towards the deserts of North Africa.

The topsails of my father's ship took me to the islands of the Caribbean, and they were beautiful. I knew them all well as I sailed them on my father's schooners. The pristine beaches and beautiful coral reefs blended with clear transparent water and are imprinted forever on my mind.

Like my father I grew up to be a man of the sea lucky to sail on some of the finest and most beautiful sailing ships afloat and I loved them.

And then there was a time when change came in my life, and I met my true love and she brought me two wonderful children. It was the fulfillment of my life.

And now as I sail towards the next chapter of my life's voyage I am again in the land of my birth where my adventure began all those years ago.

My dreams still recall faraway lands and I take the poor people of the world as my own. I feel their pain and suffering, and my heart goes out to them. They were many and of different religions and nationalities. I say without any doubt that there were many different personalities. It is my memory and belief that there is a lot of good in the world and there are a lot of good people. Those who give of themselves with kindness to help us are souls of the highest order. There are a few of the other type who would take my living heart away from me, but my way was always to try a good word and kindness. I share with you now that this is a good action and an effective one. I have tried to live my life with my palm always opened as I extend my arm not with a fist.

Today our world is in pain. There is a lot of anger and hurt. But we must all believe that over the horizon lies hope, goodness, and new life. Sail your ship to the good over the horizon and you will not be disappointed. Bring with you a cargo of kindness and love to unload at your life's ports of call. If we all practice this simple ideal, we will heal the World and make life better for all.

So, from my heart to yours I send a kind thought and wish of happiness.

Captain Lou Boudreau

About the Author

Robert Louis (Lou) Boudreau, first went to sea when he was six months old aboard the famous 98-foot schooner Yankee. His father owned and sailed the schooner in the beautiful Bras d'Or Lakes of Cape Breton, Nova Scotia, Canada. When Lou was a year old the Boudreau's left Canada and voyaged south to warmer climes. Sailing out of Miami, Florida, they eventually ran their charter cruises in the West Indies. Lou spent his early childhood on the island of St. Lucia, sailing the Caribbean aboard such vessels as the 100-foot schooner Doubloon and the 98-foot Howard Chappelle designed Baltimore clipper Caribee, both owned by his father.

The adventures under sail made a deep and lasting impression on young Lou. In 1968, at age 16, Lou joined the crew of the 135-foot Herreshoff schooner Ramona on a voyage to Nova Scotia, and following this, left school to follow the sea permanently. The young seafarer's apprenticeship saw him on some well-known sailing vessels including the 143-foot schooner Bluenose II and the 137-foot Herreshoff schooner Le Voyageur.

Over the years, Captain Lou Boudreau has experienced the exciting and the terrifying. Through hurricanes, an attempted drug hijacking in the Bahamas and a shipboard fire during a storm off the African coast, he has led the adventurer's life.

Captain Lou Boudreau

www.ingramcontent.com/pod-product-compliance
Lightning Source LLC
Chambersburg PA
CBHW070548160426
43199CB00014B/2414